Prais
Choosing
Learning to Love

MW00390446

Growing into gratitude comes in discrete pieces: coming to see "calamity" as a deepening experience, as well as recognizing that one already has enough. The culmination of this gem of a book is the account of the author's brother's learning how to say "thank you" in the face of his inevitable death. Like a slow-building formation, James Autry's wisdom regarding gratitude slowly builds into insight that repeatedly appears just when needed.

—JOHN MAGUIRE
President Emeritus
Claremont Graduate University

Jim Autry does it again. In his usual winsome and witty way, Autry reminds us that our posture toward daily life—on both good days and bad—ought to be one of gratitude. With just the right blend of humor and heart, his stories, poems, and reflections all serve to help us develop and nurture our own spirit of gratitude.

—DAVID W. MILLER
Director, Princeton University Faith & Work Initiative

Jim Autry is a very wise soul. His inspiring stories, observations, and suggestions are helpful in living a life full of gratitude. This is a very worthwhile read.

—PETER ROY
Co-author *The Book of Hard Choices*
Former President of Whole Foods Market

CHOOSING GRATITUDE
365 DAYS A YEAR

Smyth & Helwys Publishing, Inc.
6316 Peake Road
Macon, Georgia 31210-3960
1-800-747-3016
©2012 by James A. Autry
All rights reserved.
Printed in the United States of America.

The paper used in this publication meets the minimum requirements of
American National Standard for Information Sciences—
Permanence of Paper for Printed Library Materials.
ANSI Z39.48–1984. (alk. paper)

Library of Congress Cataloging-in-Publication Data

Autry, James A.
Choosing gratitude 365 days a year / by James A. Autry and Sally J. Pederson.
pages cm
ISBN 978-1-57312-689-2 (pbk. : alk. paper)
1. Gratitude. I. Title. II. Title: Choosing gratitude three hundred sixty-five days a year.
BJ1533.G8A98 2013
241'.4--dc23

2013029729

Your Daily Guide to Grateful Living

CHOOSING GRATITUDE

365 DAYS A YEAR

James A. Autry and Sally J. Pederson

We dedicate this book to our son,
Ronald, who teaches us how to live
in gratitude every day.
—JAA and SJP

Acknowledgments

So many of the daily entries in this book derive from the rich history of interactions and experiences with friends and loved ones that we must first acknowledge them (and they know who they are).

Next we acknowledge those who sent us suggestions and ideas for entries. Even the ones we did not use were valuable to us in the process of writing.

Friend Phil Hey was generous in giving permission to use his poetry, and Jeanne Cahill offered scenes from her own story for our consideration. We used several.

We acknowledge with appreciation Keith Gammons of Smyth & Helwys for his enthusiastic support from the first idea for this book to its final production, and for his welcoming of us as co-authors.

Finally, we thank our editor, Leslie Andres, who brings to her critical job not only a sharp editorial eye but also an upbeat attitude.

—JAA and SJP

Contents

Introduction

We had never considered writing a "day book," but after *Choosing Gratitude: Learning to Love the Life You Have* was published, many people wrote and e-mailed, asking for ideas and guidance for ways to live their gratitude—not merely talk about it but *live* it. Many said they were using *Choosing Gratitude* for daily meditation readings; thus we were inspired to develop a book specifically designed for people to use every day.

Gratitude is not something you're born with, it's not about doing something, and it's more than just an attitude. Gratitude is a way of being that expresses itself in your life as a spiritual practice, like meditation or centering prayer. In short, the more you nurture the spirit of gratitude, the more you live gratitude every day.

But it is not easy. It requires practice and commitment. The process begins, we believe, with simply learning to pay attention every day to how you can find gratitude in whatever you do. That's how we hope this book can help.

Our lives are so filled with burdensome activities and requirements and obligations that it's challenging to shift focus from the life "out there" to the inner life. But here's the secret: as you work to practice gratitude—and yes, it sometimes takes work—your life becomes one of gratitude. What does that mean? Simply that you become a more caring, generous, and open-minded person. At some point, even those "activities and requirements and obligations" become sources of gratitude rather than burdens.

It is important to remember, amid the problems in this world and in our lives, that there is always more reason for gratitude than for despair.

The great poet William Stafford said that the writer's work is to "dig so deep into his own story that he reaches everybody's story." In that vein, we draw on our own stories and experiences and how they inspired our gratitude. We have included several quotes and poems and added commentary that relates them to our lives.

Our hope is that you, in mining the sources of gratitude in your lives, will be moved to examine your daily experiences, your friendships, your relationships with loved ones, your deep interests, and your memories. We guarantee that this very process will become its own source of gratitude.

Incidentally, after each day's entry, you will find initials indicating which of us wrote that particular day's commentary (JAA or SJP). And, following the lead of Cicero, who wrote, "Gratitude is not only the greatest of virtues but the parent of all the others," we have chosen to offer on the first day of each month our thoughts about one of the virtues.

Finally, although these daily pages begin with January 1, there's no requirement to begin on that day. Start in March or June or whenever you acquired this book, and simply stick with the 365 days until you come around again to the date when you started.

And remember, pay attention every single day.

—James A. Autry and Sally J. Pederson

January 1

"We are constantly invited to be who we are." (Henry David Thoreau)

IT COULD BE THAT the most difficult work in life is to be authentic. What does that mean? You've heard the expression, "She's (or he's) real," or "With him (or her), what you see is what you get." Those are popular ways of describing authenticity. What makes it so difficult are all the voices urging us not to be our authentic selves, urging us to do or say or behave in accordance with the expectations of others. If we give in to those voices long enough, if we abandon our own self-defined ways of doing, saying, or behaving, we may gain the approval of others, but we will sacrifice the people we truly want to be. I think living the authentic life is about manifesting the same values in every situation and with all people.

In order to live a life of gratitude, we must first be grateful for the people we are.

Read what others have written about being real:

"The privilege of a lifetime is to become who you truly are."
(Carl G. Jung)

"No one man can, for any considerable time, wear one face to himself, and another to the multitude, without finally getting bewildered as to which is the true one."
(Nathaniel Hawthorne)

"To find yourself, think for yourself." (Socrates)

Are you the same person in all situations and with all people? If so, by all means be grateful for that.

—JAA

January 2

MY HUSBAND AND I were cleaning out an old chest of drawers when we came across a forgotten stack of handwritten letters. What a treasure trove.

The airmail letters, postmarked from Italy in 1987 through 1989, were sent to us from a couple whose corporate assignment had taken them to Parma for three years.

It was a joy to reread these letters, journaling the adventures and challenges our friends encountered in setting up hearth and home for themselves and two young children, all while learning a new language and culture. Much of the content was about everyday experiences, but poignant passages described the stress and strain involved in adjusting to a new life abroad. It was clear that our friendship and constancy was in some ways a tether for them during tumultuous times.

We visited them once while they were in Italy, and they returned to Des Moines after their three-year stint. Over the next twenty-five years, we grew to be the closest of friends, engaged in the lives of one another's children and supporting one another through life's many milestones—children's bar mitzvahs and weddings, the deaths of parents, our own birthdays and anniversaries.

None of us knows who will be our lifelong friends until we look back from the vantage point of age. But reading these letters that recounted the early years of our friendship made the likelihood of our deep, enduring bond seem inevitable.

Who are the blessed friends in your life for whom you are grateful?

—SJP

January 3

THE YOGI PARAMAHANSA YOGANANDA wrote that we should be positive and try to be cheerful to the last day of our lives. This is much easier said than done, of course. We can't just take a cheerful pill, and we are surrounded by heaps of bad news in the media every day. How do we do it? We start in ways that, in themselves, are not easy. Some people meditate, some people pray, some people do both. Some people simply try to do everyday things meditatively without a prescribed routine. Some people are moved to cheerfulness by the antics of children or birds or animals. Some people bring cheer to one another through friendship and fellowship. Adopting a positive attitude about life and the world is not always easy, but it's worth the effort, and I think it begins with an attitude of gratitude.

Can you be positive and cheerful today because of—or despite—the world and its pleasures or pressures?

—JAA

January 4

SOME DAYS ARE HARDER than others, and it seems that the more we try to do, the less we get done. That leads to discouragement and sometimes even depression. The first step back to balance and contentment may be to stop trying so hard and, as they say in Alcoholics Anonymous, "Let go and let God." The great Sufi poet Rumi put it this way:

"You are so weak. Give up to grace.
The ocean takes care of each wave till it gets to shore.
You need more help than you know." (from *The Essential Rumi*)

Are you finding it hard to live in gratitude today? Try letting go of all you think you should be doing, sit quietly, and let grace take over.

—JAA

January 5

HERE'S AN EXERCISE: List seven people to whom you want to express gratitude this week, and then do it, one a day, one day at a time. This will help you focus on gratitude all week. These expressions can be as simple as calling a relative you've not talked with in a while or greeting and thanking your mail carrier.

If, like many people, you keep a gratitude journal, this exercise can help you move those writings into action.

Make this a practice in the first week of each month and see if you don't appreciate life more.

—JAA

January 6

I GET TOGETHER WITH five other women to celebrate our birthdays over a cup of coffee and a pastry. We meet in January, May, July, September, and November. (Two of us share the January celebration.)

When we started this ritual as young mothers in the 1980s, none of us could have imagined we would still be doing it almost three decades later. That's a lot of birthdays under the bridge.

Over the course of those nearly thirty years, we have shared much more than happy birthday wishes—a divorce, a son's tragic death, anniversaries, children's weddings, job losses, cancer treatments, and parents' passing. The difficult and painful times were made more bearable by the support we gave one another; the joys of our journeys were multiplied and sweetened by sharing.

Who would have guessed that such rich and enduring friendships could have grown from simply sharing birthday cards over coffee?

Is there someone to whom you should send a birthday greeting of gratitude today?

—SJP

January 7

"Two kinds of gratitude: the sudden kind we feel for what we take; the larger kind we feel for what we give." (Edwin Arlington Robinson)

IT TOOK ME A while to understand the old saying that giving is better than receiving. I think it happened when I finally comprehended that those to whom we give something—money, goods, or love—are offering us that privilege by their willingness to accept something from us.

Do you feel privileged and grateful when you give to others?

—JAA

January 8

BASIC JET-FIGHTER PILOT TRAINING in the early stages is, as much as anything, a lot about practicing mistakes so you'll know how to avoid them or how to correct them. My first night flight was on a dark, moonless night. We were over west Texas, and the lights on the ground could easily have been mistaken for stars. My instructor put me through some maneuvers to assure that I could learn to avoid becoming disoriented. Toward the end of the flight, he said, "Close your eyes," and then he rolled the airplane to an inverted position. Then he said, "Open your eyes. You have the airplane." I put my hand on the control stick. We were losing altitude, so I pulled back on the stick. We lost more altitude. Then I realized that we were inverted, so I quickly rolled out, to my instructor's satisfaction.

But that's not what I remember most. I remember how much the lights on the ground looked like stars and vice versa and how delighted I was to be hanging there as if suspended between heaven and earth. I would not have used this word then, but it was wondrous.

You don't have to be in a jet to feel suspended between heaven and earth. You can get the same feeling by living in gratitude.

—JAA

January 9

WE AWOKE TO AN early winter storm last year that brought several feet of snow and closed schools and many businesses. The electricity went out in our neighborhood, and it was clear from the start that we weren't going anywhere that day. We had no idea how long our furnace would be out, so we put on an extra layer of clothing, built a fire in the living room fireplace, and snuggled in for the duration.

Most of our lives revolve around things that operate on electricity—radios, televisions, laptops, iPads, cell phones. The idea that those constant connections to the outside world no longer worked or might actually run out of energy was suddenly very real.

We found that we liked the opportunity to be isolated and excused from the onslaught of daily busyness. The gas stove was still working, so we had the luxury of hot coffee and tea, and we soon settled in to watch the fire and enjoy the blanket of quiet that had covered our lives.

Can a disruption in your scheduled life be an opportunity for quiet reflection? Are you grateful when nature offers a chance to unplug from your routine?

—SJP

January 10

MY MOTHER STUDIED ART in school but never got much time to paint until later in her life. At some point, she gave up still lifes and landscapes and such, and focused on scenes from her childhood. The walls of my home now are hung with paintings of a "quilting bee," "wash day," "sorghum making," "cotton picking," and "baptizing in the river," along with others. I am grateful not only for these wonderful paintings but also for my late mother's art and life.

Are there creative efforts of a friend or loved one for which you are grateful today?

—JAA

January 11

"Learn to . . . be what you are, and learn to resign with good grace all that you are not." (Henri Frederic Amiel)

"**WHAT YOU SEE IS** what you get with him."

"She's real."

These are ways of describing a person who is authentic, who is consistently the same person wherever she is or whatever he's doing. Authentic people are recognizable because they always exhibit the same virtues and manifest the same values. And you can be sure that authentic people live a life of gratitude.

Think about your life today. How do you think others would describe you? If they say you're real and that what they see is what they get with you, then be grateful for how you have chosen to live your life.

—JAA

January 12

IN GOING THROUGH AN old trunk belonging to my late mother, I came across a stack of diaries that covered several years. They were written by my late stepfather, a gentle man, schoolteacher, and self-directed scholar. I started looking through them and found that the entry for every day—every day!—began with these words: "This is the day the Lord hath made; let us rejoice and be glad in it." You may recognize those words from the 118th Psalm. It strikes me that beginning every day by rejoicing is the same as beginning every day in the spirit of gratitude.

Rejoice today and be grateful.

—JAA

January 13

MY HUSBAND AND MY mother share a natural green thumb. One aspect of their talent is the exceptional ability to coax a second, third, and even tenth bloom out of houseplants that most of us give up on after the original blossoms fade.

Two plants that currently reside on a table in front of the window in my home office are coming back to life right now.

The Christmas cactus came from a cutting from my mother's ancient plant. While the outside temperature hovers at 3 degrees, this transplanted specimen brightens my room with hot pink bursts of color.

Beside it sits an orchid held over from last March—my gift to Jim on his birthday. Over the past several months, I have watched it sprout a new stem with seven buds that will soon begin to open.

Growing up, I watched with amazement as my mother nursed fading plants back to thriving vegetation, but for some reason I didn't inherit her horticultural inclinations. Fortunately, I married a green-thumbed gardener who happily shares his blooming rehabbed treasures with me.

Are there people in your life who nurture what others are ready to abandon?

—SJP

January 14

"There's no such thing in anyone's life as an unimportant day." (Alexander Woollcott)

I STILL FALL INTO the trap of coming to the end of a day and thinking, "I didn't get done what I'd planned to do today." That attitude deprives me of recognizing what I did accomplish that day. And it could have been that I "accomplished" nothing that could be counted in a traditional way; perhaps I took a nap or read the paper or took a walk or just sat and watched the birds. Those things would make the day just as important as any other day, no matter how full of "accomplishment" the day might have been. If there needs to be a measure of a day's importance, I remind myself that living in gratitude for this very day is the measure.

Can you live in gratitude for this day, whatever it brings?

—JAA

January 15

IT SEEMS TO ME that the difference between gifts and offerings is that we give gifts because we hope they will make the recipient happy. We give offerings because we care enough about the recipient that we want to make a connection by sharing something that has meaning to us. The difference is not in the act of giving but in what it represents. That distinction became clear to me recently when an acquaintance gave me an old hymnal. She is a person who worked hard all her life, is now retired, and is of modest means. Knowing that I had written a book on gratitude, she'd carefully underlined "gratitude" wherever it appeared in two hymns she'd found. I realized this required some effort, and I tried to express my gratitude, but I confess that my words seemed meager compared to the blessing of her offering.

Be grateful if you have been blessed by the offerings of others.

—JAA

January 16

WHEN I SEE MAGAZINE photos of contemporary rooms in which everything is in its place and the walls and tabletops are empty and uncluttered, I wonder who could possibly live there. Our house has photos and objects and memorabilia in almost every space. I love to walk around and let my eye fall where it will. This morning it fell on a close-up photograph that a photographer friend took of a garden spider. Imagine that—a garden spider. But it's a beautiful photo, and it hangs in my "mud room," where I wash up after being in the garden. I find myself grateful for the photographer friend, grateful for the photograph, and grateful for the garden spider.

Walk around your living space and note the little things that inspire your gratitude today.

—JAA

January 17

"Never blame any day in your life. Good days give you happiness. Bad days give you experience." (author unknown)

LIKE EVERYONE ELSE, I sometimes take a dualistic view of the world. Things are good or bad, black or white, true or false. This attitude always accompanies the temptation to be judgmental, which, combined with the dualism, works against living a life of gratitude. Gratitude is sometimes hard work because I have to make myself realize that everything counts, every day counts, every experience counts, and I have to be grateful for it all.

Be grateful for all your days, including this one.

—JAA

January 18

A HAND-PAINTED GOLDEN sunflower on a blue-green background decorates a wooden plaque that sits in a place of honor in our home. Etched in script below the upturned face of the flower are these words: *Turn your face to the sun and the shadows fall behind you.*

The beautifully crafted piece was a gift from my friend, Joanne Johnson, a talented artist and a wise and generous soul. She gave it to me years ago—perhaps for a birthday, though I don't remember which one.

I pass this cheery painting dozens of times each day and think of the verse as both a compliment and an admonition. I'm flattered that my friend sees me as a person who looks on life with optimism and hope, but I also am grateful for the daily reminder her artwork so gently offers.

In what ways will you look ahead with optimism and gratitude today and leave the shadows behind?

—SJP

January 19

ONE OF THE MOST important things I've learned is the power of silence. In working with management groups in all kinds of organizations, I've used times of silence to urge people to move from a frame of mind focused on what to say next to a peaceful state in which they try to let go of their natural urges to "do something" and instead just "be." It has become more and more difficult in our world to sit in silence, but I have found it to be therapeutic balm for the spirit. When I take time to sit quietly, gratitude becomes a part of my consciousness.

Try sitting quietly for ten minutes today, thinking of nothing but the things for which you are grateful.

—JAA

January 20

I GREW UP IN THE segregated South, went to segregated public schools in Memphis, and graduated from the segregated University of Mississippi. The truth is, until I went to college, I didn't think much about race. Like a lot of Southern teenagers, I guess I just accepted segregation as the way things were. In college, the whole ugly picture came into focus, and I joined a group of journalism students who supported integration of the university. But it was not to be for another decade. When I moved to Iowa, I was hesitant to say that the University of Mississippi was my alma mater. In those years, I tried hard not to be a white Southerner. Dr. Martin Luther King, Jr., raised my consciousness about the pervasive racism all around me—yes, even in the company where I worked and the northern community where I lived.

Dr. King raised that consciousness for a lot of people, and as we remember him, I am grateful for his life and work.

Join me today in gratitude for the life of Dr. King and all people of all colors who still work for racial justice.

—JAA

January 21

"Take the first step in faith. You don't have to see the whole staircase, just take the first step." (Martin Luther King, Jr.)

Dr. King's words join the great body of wisdom literature that reminds us that change only happens when we take action, however small, to make a difference. Each day is a new opportunity to make a small difference.

Like every journey, the path to a life of gratitude begins with one step. Be grateful for this very moment in time.

—SJP

January 22

IT'S COMMON TO SEE a jigsaw puzzle, in some state of assembly, on the table in our library. Our son Ronald loves to work on puzzles and does so with laser-like concentration. He seldom tackles any with fewer than 1,000 pieces. One time he spent an entire year meticulously assembling a life-sized grandfather clock with thousands of deep mahogany-colored pieces and an actual working clock.

When Ronald was young, he would object if anyone tried to join him. But now he often asks me to help with the puzzle, and we visit in a relaxed manner while we work. Ronald's method is trial and error, simply fitting one piece against another until he gets a match. I study the photo on the box and look for pieces according to the picture. I don't think my system is any faster than his, but our minds work differently. Considering that he has autism and I do not, that is no surprise. Yet it strikes me that our different approach to solving jigsaw puzzles is a metaphor for the different ways our brains perceive the world—I can see the big picture; Ronald is focused on an intricate detail without making sense of the whole. Is it any wonder that the logo used by the Autism Society of America and Autism Speaks is a lone puzzle piece?

The human puzzles in our lives can be rich with wonder and joy. Be grateful for the things that are beyond our earthly understanding.

—SJP

January 23

"The real voyage of discovery consists not in seeking new landscapes, but in having new eyes." (Marcel Proust)

THIS TIME OF YEAR, I long for a seaside vacation, an escape from the snow and ice of the Midwest winter. Yet, sometimes, all I really need is to take an adult education class, volunteer for a just cause, attend a stimulating lecture, or read a really good book.

Today, engage in life in a new way and open your eyes to new discoveries.

—SJP

January 24

A FEW YEARS AGO, as an elder of my church, I had an experience that filled me with gratitude. My job was to deliver Communion to older people who could no longer make it to church. "Shut-ins," they're commonly called. What I experienced was a different kind of Communion, a Communion that was not intended but that became a great blessing to me as the day passed. After the wine and bread ceremony, it became clear that the people did not want me to leave. I realized that each elderly person, in his or her eager looks, was saying, "I have a story, I have a story. Listen to me." So I listened, and our Communion took on a wholly and holy different dimension.

Can you find opportunities to be a listener today? Someone you know has a story to tell, and you'll be grateful when you hear it.

—JAA

January 25

IN HER WONDERFUL POEM "Famous," my friend, the poet Naomi Shihab Nye, closed with these lines:

> I want to be famous in the way a pulley is famous,
> or a buttonhole, not because it did anything spectacular,
> but because it never forgot what it did.

There are so many everyday things that do what they do without recognition, and we take them for granted because they've always been there and we've always been able to depend on them.

If you think about it, you can probably name at least ten common things for which you are grateful. Try doing that today.

—JAA

January 26

I CONFESS THAT I am often guilty of taking my blessings for granted. I think it's because I don't stop to identify the daily blessings as they appear. Perhaps it's that I subconsciously think of them as "little blessings," such as an e-mail from an old friend or even something new blooming in my greenhouse. I have to tell myself consciously, "There are no little blessings, you fool. All blessings are important, and you need to count them as they are revealed." So I resolve to do that today.

Join me today in an act of gratitude, and let's count our blessings.

—JAA

January 27

I AM ALWAYS ON the search for the perfect scone and the perfect biscotti, sampling them at coffee shops whenever they look authentically homemade. My friend, Joanne, discovered an excellent recipe and gave me a copy along with a generous batch she had made.

I long ago finished off the last of her most excellent biscotti, and I have been waiting for an uninterrupted afternoon to try my hand at the new recipe.

Today was that day.

I toasted the almonds, measured out the dry ingredients, and was about to whip the eggs, when I discovered that the last two eggs in the carton were past their freshness date. I quickly dashed to the store to pick up a fresh dozen.

When I opened the back door and walked into the kitchen, I was engulfed in the thick, rich aroma of roasted almonds. I hadn't noticed their powerful fragrance permeating the house while I was toasting them—it had all come on so gradually. Now, stepping into the room from the crisp winter air, I was overcome by the delicious smell.

Today, pay attention to your senses—taste, touch, sight, smell, hearing— and be grateful for the wondrous way in which you are able to take in the world around you.

—SJP

CHOOSING GRATITUDE

January 28

A POPULAR ADMONITION IS *carpe diem,* "seize the day." I never thought much about it until I realized that it is part of our preoccupation with action. I once heard a speaker say, "Don't just do something, sit there!" It made me question all the constant activity so many of us seem to seek.

Rather than "seize the day," how about "embrace the day"? Isn't that more appealing?

If you're really busy today, consider taking a little time to embrace the day with gratitude.

—JAA

January 29

LIKE MOST MIDWESTERNERS, I complain about the winter weather, but actually I find a day like today to be one of my favorites of the year.

The sun was shining, the temperature was just a little above freezing, and the six inches of snow we had received two days earlier had been cleared from most roads and sidewalks.

It was a perfect day to walk the dog with my son, Ronald. His corgi, Gilda, has a thick fur coat built for this weather, and she delights in romping through the snow on her stubby little legs with her mouth cocked open, skimming the topmost layer of fluff as she goes.

Sometimes we make snowballs and throw them for Gilda to fetch. She dutifully chases them as they disappear into the field of white and then comes up with a mouthful of snow.

Ron and I laugh and Gilda barks. Such simple pleasures!

What simple pleasures are you grateful for on this winter day?

—SJP

January 30

"Happy is the person who doesn't show hatred over what is lost, but shows gratefulness over what is left." (author unknown)

IN THIS UNPREDICTABLE WORLD with its political and economic problems, I realize that I must put my energy into being grateful for what *is* rather than bemoaning what *is not*. And I must pass this attitude along to my children and to anyone else who will listen. This is the only way to nurture gratitude in the face of fear and uncertainty about potential losses and setbacks.

Can you let gratitude be your response to the uncertainties of this world?

—JAA

January 31

"CARING FOR ONE ANOTHER, we sometimes glimpse an essential quality of our being. We may be sitting alone, lost in self-doubt or self-pity, when the phone rings with a call from a friend who's really depressed. Instinctively, we come out of ourselves, just to be there with her and say a few reassuring words. When we're done, and a little comfort's been shared, we put down the phone and feel a little more at home with ourselves. We're reminded of who we really are and what we have to offer one another." (from Ram Dass, *How Can I Help?*)

Be grateful for those who help others, and be grateful for your own willingness to help.

—JAA

February 1

THINK ABOUT KINDNESS TODAY. We can't keep kindness to ourselves, because kindness is a virtue that is always expressed toward others. We should be grateful when people are willing to be treated with kindness, but we also should not expect the reward of their gratitude. Kindness is its own reward. And don't confuse kindness with generosity. Generosity is about what we give to others, and kindness is about how we interact with others.

Read these thoughts on kindness:

"For kindness begets kindness evermore . . ." (Sophocles)

"Kindness is the language which the deaf can hear and the blind can see." (Mark Twain)

"That best portion of a good man's life,
His little, nameless, unremembered acts
Of Kindness and of Love." (Wordsworth)

"Have you had a kindness shown? Pass it on." (Henry Burton)

"And be ye kind, one to another . . ." (Ephesians 4:32, KJV)

"No act of kindness, however small, is ever wasted." (Aesop)

Be grateful for a life that inspires you to commit random acts of kindness.
—JAA

February 2

I HAVE A DEAR friend, David Jordan, with whom I worked in the magazine business for more than thirty years. We started at the same company within six months of one another. He was a former Navy officer; I was a former Air Force officer. David is extraordinarily talented and also a decent and compassionate human being. A few years ago, I learned that he was volunteering in the neonatal unit of a local hospital. His job: to hold the babies from time to time. I asked him about it. "Some of these babies," he said, "don't have any family that comes to hold them, and newborns need that connection. The hospital people don't have enough time to do it all, so I try to help."

I was very moved by the image of this large man holding such tiny babies in their tenuous grasp on life, and I felt grateful that he was doing it.

Take time to say a prayer of gratitude for the people who work to help the helpless.

—JAA

February 3

"Gratitude can turn a negative into a positive. Find a way to be thankful for your troubles, and they can become your blessings." (author unknown)

IN OUR SOCIETY, with its great emphasis on accomplishment and success, it is particularly difficult to grasp the concept of being grateful for our troubles. I once made a sizable and costly mistake in business. I went to my boss and offered to resign. He said, "Absolutely not. We just spent a lot of money on your training." I realized then that my mistake had become a blessing and that I would never make that mistake, or one like it, again.

Can you find the blessings in the midst of your troubles?

—JAA

February 4

A COUPLE OF YEARS ago, I was invited to speak at the annual awards banquet of Goodwill Industries of Central Iowa. In the process of preparing my remarks, I learned the interesting history of the organization.

The founder, Edgar Helms, was born in 1863 and grew up on a 100-acre farm in rural Iowa. No doubt, he learned the Midwestern values of hard work and good neighbors in those early years on the family farm. After high school, he attended Cornell College in Mt. Vernon, Iowa, where he earned a degree in philosophy and the highest grades ever given a student at Cornell. He went on to Boston University to receive training as a Methodist minister.

The Reverend Helms was then assigned to a church in one of the poorest and most crime-ridden neighborhoods of Boston. There he found an overwhelming need for food and clothing. So Helms began a system of collecting used items from the wealthy families of Boston society and repairing them for resale to the poor.

It was an idea that worked. Today, Goodwill Industries provides education, training, employment, and clothing to make a difference to millions of people across the country and around the world.

I am grateful for the vision and passion of people like Edgar Helms. What visionary leader has made a difference in your life?

—SJP

February 5

WE WERE SNOWED IN a few weeks ago and lost electrical power. Thus our fireplace, which is mostly for show, became a needed source of heat.

With no TV, no Internet, and no good reading lights, we found ourselves just sitting, talking, and watching the fire.

It took me back to the years when a fireplace was never for show but was the only source of heat, when my dad had to get up early every morning and stoke up the fire, add large "sticks of firewood," as he called them, then go build a fire in the cook stove and put on the coffee. Only after that would I pull myself from under the quilts and rush with my clothes to dress in front of the fireplace.

During the summer every year, we had to cut and stack enough firewood to last through the cold season. When I was about twelve years old, Dad paid me fifteen cents to help him fell a tree with a big two-man, crosscut saw, and then a penny for each large section we cut. Later, he'd split those sections into firewood, and we'd stack them.

Now I buy my firewood, and the only work involved is bringing it inside when I'm ready to use it.

I am grateful for those memories of earlier days, of cutting and stacking the firewood. And I'm very grateful that I don't have to do it anymore.

What memories do you treasure of chores or activities that you're also glad you don't have to do now?

—JAA

CHOOSING GRATITUDE

February 6

"MOM," HE SAID IN a plaintive voice, "I couldn't help myself. I went to Walgreens and bought a bunch of candy."

This wasn't the first time Ronald had called, confessing his overindulgence and subsequent guilty conscience, after backsliding on his diet.

Keeping away from sweets is a real challenge for him, and he needs lots of support to keep his weight and cholesterol numbers under control.

"I need help," he says. And I am grateful he asks for it.

The difference between his intention to eat a healthy diet and his willpower to resist all those fat- and sugar-laden goodies lining the shelves of grocery stores, convenience shops, and pharmacies reminds me of how "normal" he is in his essential human nature despite his autism.

He also reminds me that asking for help isn't a weakness—it's a strength, because in the end we are all simply human.

Who helps you when you need support? Are you grateful when you can help others?

—SJP

February 7

A FRIEND WRITES THAT she is "grateful for the birds at the feeder outside the kitchen window, little miracles that give color, movement, and music in return for a bag of sunflower seeds. Their cheery antics start my day with joy."

Are you grateful for these simple pleasures that start your day with joy?

—JAA

February 8

A BIG STORM'S COMING in this evening, bringing with it not only a foot of snow but lots of questions. From the kids: will the schools be closed—we hope, we hope? From working people: will my workplace be closed, will the buses run, and will the streets be cleared?

There is much activity. Grocery stores are packed with shoppers, and for some reason, restaurants are doing a strong business. The mood seems almost celebratory. The TV weather people are as happy as can be. And of course, the snowplows will soon be busy clearing the streets to keep the city moving.

Join me in gratitude for this energy and all the people who work so hard to help us cope with nature.

—JAA

February 9

I'M NOT A SLAVE to routine, but I depend on routines in my daily life. They keep me focused and organized, much as my checklists did when I was flying jets in the Air Force years ago. Some of the daily routines, such as exercise and meditation and a quiet time with my wife at the end of the day, transcend routine and grow into rituals. They then take on special meaning and become important daily touchstones of gratitude for the everydayness of life itself.

For which everyday routines or rituals of your life are you most grateful?

—JAA

February 10

MY DAD LIKES TO tell a story about his grandfather's reaction the first time he ever saw a television in 1948. Great-grandpa Tharp was born in the 1880s, so you can imagine the changes he had seen in his lifetime.

Our family was one of the first to own a TV in our town, and it was quite a novelty. Grandpa Tharp looked at the snowy picture on the TV screen and said, "I don't know how they do that, but then I don't suppose anybody really does."

I feel that way sometimes when I look at all the amazing things that my new phone can do, from tracking airplanes and packages to translating French. The other day, my four-year-old grandnephew, Reid, taught me how to take videos with my iPad. What a world we live in!

Do you marvel at the fast pace of change in your world, and are you grateful that someone somewhere had the genius to invent these remarkable technologies?

—SJP

February 11

IN MY LATE BROTHER'S book, *Heaven Inc.*, he wrote that the only resource on which God placed no limit is love. Thus, we are able to do as the theologian John Shelby Spong suggests and "love wastefully," because if there is no limit on love, it cannot be wasted.

Can you be so trusting of others that you can love wastefully? If so, be grateful today for that gift.

—JAA

February 12

I'M SORT OF A fanatic about not throwing anything away. I have boxes of stuff—letters, memos, calendars, old magazines, random photographs, etc.—very little of which is filed and organized. My wife refers to all this as the "Autry Archives," and I know that when I pass on, this stuff will be designated for the recycler. Meanwhile, I dive into it every once in a while with the same kind of curiosity an archaeologist might have, and with the determination to discard a large quantity of it. I start digging, and then I fall into reading and inevitably come across something that stirs my gratitude, like a personal note or a newspaper clipping, and I find myself putting things right back where I got them, with the comment, "I might need that someday."

Do you have in your closet or files or drawers a collection of memories that stirs your gratitude? This might be a good day to dive into them.

—JAA

February 13

"Remember, people will judge you by your actions, not your intentions. You may have a heart of gold, but so does a hard-boiled egg." (anonymous)

I'VE ALWAYS HEARD THE saying that the road to hell is paved with good intentions, but I continue to have many things I intend to do or say that don't get done or said. My excuse is time, but I am grateful for this quote that reminds me that nothing should demand my time as much as my acts of kindness or my words of comfort or praise. Good intentions are not enough.

Think about something you've intended to do or say, and make time for it today. You'll be grateful you did.

—JAA

February 14

THE NEWSPAPER REPORTED THAT a local woman had just bought a bag full of Valentine cards to add to the dozen she'd already mailed. Most of us probably consider Valentine's Day something of a minor holiday, but this woman makes it into an expression of gratitude.

She said, "It's just a time to stop and think about how lucky I am to have such great friends and relatives and loved ones."

A worthy thought for all of us.

Today, be grateful for your great friends and relatives. (And there's still time to get some cards in the mail.)

—JAA

February 15

IN LATE FEBRUARY, MY parents flew from Iowa to Arizona to spend a week with relatives. At ages ninety-two and eighty-seven, Mom and Dad still have great exuberance for life. Here's the e-mail my mother sent out upon their return:

"Home again!! Home again! Safely and joyfully(!) from a very excellent vacation in Az. and visit with relatives Marlyn and Larry and Kathleen. Details when we see you. Love always, Mom"

Who are your role models for living with an attitude of gratitude?

—SJP

February 16

ONE OF MY DEAR friends and a fellow former fighter pilot had a cattle business several years ago, and I always delighted in the way he watched the seasons and in his generally upbeat attitude. In what seemed to me the dead of winter with subzero temperatures and snow on the ground, he'd look at me with a big grin and say something like, "Only six more weeks to grass and eight more weeks to calving time." I was grateful for the way he lifted his friends' spirits with those optimistic prognostications.

Today, think about how your optimistic attitude can lift the spirits of someone you know.

—JAA

February 17

THERE WAS A FAMILY gathering recently to celebrate two birthdays, mine and my ninety-two-year-old father-in-law's. As a light-hearted touch, I pulled my Air Force uniform from its place of honor in the closet. I hadn't worn it in over forty years. It still fit. I've always worked to maintain my weight as one way to stay healthy, but wearing that uniform to the party was not about health; it was about ego. I have to admit that strutting around in the same uniform I wore as a young man was good for my spirits. Now there's something for which to be grateful!

Do you still get a kick out of doing things that give you pride in your accomplishments?

—JAA

February 18

OUR FAMILY SPENT A WEEK this winter on the Gulf Coast of Florida to get away from the snow and ice. One evening, we were driving down the coastal highway on our way to a seaside restaurant just as the sun was setting.

The western sky began to take on a pink hue that grew deeper as the sun sank lower in the sky. As we drove, we watched the colors intensify, and soon the entire horizon was fire red. We pulled off the road and joined others at a scenic spot where people were gathering to witness this stunningly beautiful light show.

A couple had walked out on the beach, and their black silhouettes were surrounded by the brilliant red and flamingo sky. It was breathtakingly magical. We pulled out our cell phones to try to capture the wondrous sight.

Of course, looking at the photos later, we were disappointed in what they had recorded. The pictures could only act as reminders of what we'd had the great good fortune to experience. As they say, "You had to be there."

Do you stop to appreciate the daily wonders in nature? Are you fully present to the beauty of the universe revealed in the movement of the sun, the moon, the stars? Today, be grateful for the opportunity to witness these things.

—SJP

February 19

WE LIVE IN AN increasingly angry world and society. But I decided about twenty-five years ago that I could live my life without anger in business, in community life, and in personal relationships. This does not mean that I never get angry; it means that I try never to let it get the best of me. It seems to me that some people become their anger to the point that their acquaintances simply think of them as angry people. That's what I mean by letting anger get the best of you (or me). Taking three deep breaths helps. So does this quote by Mahatma Gandhi:

"I know, to banish anger altogether from one's breast is a difficult task. It cannot be achieved through pure personal effort. It can be done only by God's grace."

If you are feeling angry today, take three deep breaths and call on God's grace. If you are not feeling angry today, take three deep breaths and call on God's grace anyway.

—JAA

February 20

FROM A FRIEND: "People will forget what you said. People will forget what you did. But people will never forget how you made them feel."

This rang true to me because of my experience in management and leadership. I know that people can feel humiliated by their manager's words or feel grateful for their manager's praise. Either way, the feeling the words caused will not be forgotten.

Have you been grateful for the ways a friend, a colleague, a boss, or an employee made you feel?

—JAA

February 21

MY OLDER BROTHER, DENNY, got wind of the fact that I had taken my sister to lunch for her birthday. Of course, he wanted equal treatment.

So today I introduced him to a new neighborhood restaurant and picked up the check. We had lots to talk about—our parents, our siblings, nephews, nieces, grandchildren—and how fleeting time seems from our perch of sixty-plus years.

I don't remember the last time Denny and I had lunch together— just the two of us. Maybe a decade ago or more.

Surely we won't let that much time go by before we do it again. I might even call him, since it's his turn to buy lunch.

Today, call a sibling or close friend who'd appreciate an invitation to lunch or coffee.

—SJP

February 22

"The ornament of a house is the friends who frequent it." (Ralph Waldo Emerson)

NOTHING MAKES ME APPRECIATE my home more intensely than when good friends visit. Nothing is truer than the old saw that it takes a heap of living to make a house a home, and nothing creates a heap of living like a gathering of people who care about one other. I am grateful for the friends who can make themselves at home, be casual and natural in behavior and conversation, and feel that while they are here, our house is their house. Sometimes in the midst of a pleasant evening, I look around at my friends and think of that wonderful line from Mr. Pickwick's Christmas, "This is, indeed, comfort."

Be grateful for friends who add to your own "heap of living."

—JAA

February 23

I HAVE A FRIEND whose husband is some years older than she. He's still relatively healthy physically but is struggling with dementia. I was very moved recently when she wrote that her husband always wants to be in the same room with her and that he sleeps better and more comfortably when she is in the bed with him. This is a lesson in gratitude, and it reaffirms my belief that we become imprinted with the familiar, with ritual, and with intimacy, and that those become so much of who we are and, in turn, become so important to our well-being that, without them, we begin to decline.

Be aware that your very presence may someday be the source of gratitude for a loved one.

—JAA

February 24

MY MOTHER NEVER WENT to college, but she was an exceptional student—enough so that she was hired to teach in a one-room school in rural Missouri during the 1940s. I suspect she was a very good teacher.

She has never lost her love of learning, so she participates in groups and organizations that continue to challenge her mind and her thinking. She is a frequent visitor to the local library and over the years has introduced each of her grandchildren to its many wonders.

I am always interested to learn what she is reading, and we delight in exchanging and discussing books with one another. It is a wonderful way to share our thoughts and ideas and a reminder that we both grow and change.

Be grateful for those among your friends and family with whom you share a love of learning.

—SJP

February 25

"Farther along we'll know all about it,
Farther along we'll understand why;
Cheer up, my brother, live in the sunshine,
We'll understand it all by and by."

THESE OPTIMISTIC LINES FROM the old hymn, "Farther Along," always make me smile. My late brother loved to sing gospel music and would often gather with friends and sing late into the evening. He also had a sometimes devilish sense of humor. In this particular hymn, when he reached the phrase, "Cheer up, my brother," he would jump flat-footed from his standing position as high in the air as he could, probably less than a foot, without cracking a smile and continue to sing as if nothing happened. It could be a sometimes startling but always joyful experience for the group.

Do you allow yourself to be grateful for silly things? It's healthy.

—JAA

February 26

"WALKING THE TALK" IS a popular expression to describe people who do what they say they will do or who act on what they say they believe.

This is what is meant by "living in gratitude." President Kennedy put it best: "As we express our gratitude, we must never forget that the highest appreciation is not to utter words, but to live by them."

Think of some way today to show your gratitude, not just talk about it.

—JAA

February 27

"The bitterest tears shed over graves are for words unsaid and deeds left undone." (Harriet Beecher Stowe)

REGRET IS A WASTED EMOTION unless it moves us to rectify what we regret. It's the old curse of "woulda, coulda, shoulda," of what we did or failed to do, what we said or failed to say. In every one of these situations, the time comes when it is too late to do anything about them, and at that point it is meaningless to live in regret. I think a life of gratitude leads us to appreciate whatever opportunities we have to make amends for whatever we regret, and if there is no longer the opportunity, then we get a chance to leave regret behind with the resolve simply to learn the lesson and do better next time.

Is there anything you regret today? Think about what you might do or say so that you can leave the regret behind and focus on gratitude.

—JAA

February 28

DEEP IN THE MISSISSIPPI woods, in the Holly Springs National Forest, is the grave of my great-great-grandfather Jacob Autry. He is buried not far from land that used to be our family land. I don't know how it got to be national forest, but I suspect it had something to do with the Great Depression. Several years ago, I was asked by a cousin to contribute to a marker for the grave. I did so.

I am grateful for two things: one is that the land belongs to the American people and did not get sucked up into a commercial development; the other is that there are family people who care enough about this old resting place that they take care of it.

Are there family memorials for which you are grateful?

—JAA

March 1

HERE ARE SOME THOUGHTS about humility as we begin another month.

A person who says, "I am a humble person," probably isn't. And that person probably does not live in gratitude, because humility is the foundation of gratitude. Humility means accepting that whoever we have become, whatever we have done, and wherever we are going on life's journey are not measures of our efforts alone, but also are manifestations of the love and support of others, plus a large portion of grace. Thus, our humility reflects our attitude of gratitude.

Here's a sample of the many writings about humility:

"Before honor is humility." (Proverbs 15:33)

"The only wisdom we can hope to acquire is the wisdom of humility; humility is endless." (T. S. Eliot)

"It was pride that changed angels into devils; it is humility that makes men as angels." (Saint Augustine)

"Humility is the most difficult of all virtues to achieve; nothing dies harder than the desire to think well of oneself." (Shakespeare)

Think about the truly humble people you know or have known. Do others think of you as having humility?

—JAA

March 2

IT CAME AS A shock a few years ago when the first of my college sorority sisters died at the age of fifty-nine. Suddenly, our class had an important reason to get in touch with one another. In the intervening years we had scattered across the country, and many of us hadn't connected in decades. As you might imagine, the Internet was a big help in reaching out to find everyone.

The sad news of a classmate's death was sobering to us and prompted plans for a reunion the following year. We arranged to spend a weekend at our sorority house, congregating around the piano in the living room, sharing breakfast in the dining room, and sleeping in the dormers. I hadn't seen most of these women in twenty-five years, and at first I didn't even recognize them. But after a little conversation, their faces began to look familiar again, and I soon felt the years melt away.

I didn't organize the reunion, and it would have been easy not to go. After all, I had moved on and didn't think I could have much in common with these women from my past. But I would have missed a rich experience. They and the formative years we shared are part of who I am today, and I am grateful for that. The reunion was not an attempt to recapture lost friendships but a tribute to our shared past and the importance of those experiences in our lives at the time.

You may not be able to maintain every relationship throughout your life, but you can honor important friendships from your past and feel gratitude for them.

—SJP

March 3

AS MANY PEOPLE DO, I feed the birds in winter, and my backyard is well populated when snow covers the ground. I get a kick out of watching the little creatures and noting their feeding times. Each has a separate time, except for sparrows, who seem to feed constantly. The cardinals gather at the end of the day, and it's not unusual to see nine pairs of cardinals at the feeder.

If I'm not otherwise occupied, I watch for them every day. I consider them my own college of cardinals and wonder if they'll choose a pope one of these days.

What simple everyday antics by your feathery friends give you reasons for a grateful smile?

—JAA

March 4

I AM EIGHTY YEARS old, and in the past couple of years I have developed a friendship with a thirty-two-year-old musician. He and I met at a community arts event where he was performing and I was reading poetry. He suggested that we do some events together, with him playing and singing and me reading. We don't draw much of an audience, but we've enjoyed doing our own kind of art together, and we plan to continue. Meanwhile, we learn from each other's very different life experiences. I am grateful for this spring/December friendship, and I am grateful for how participating in the arts can bring people together.

Are there new friends or experiences for which you are grateful today?

—JAA

March 5

AFTER ALMOST TWENTY-FIVE YEARS, I recently renewed my relationship with an old friend, Marsha.

She was a high school classmate, and although we had been quite close for a few years after college, we had not seen much of each other during the past two decades.

Marsha and I now get together for lunch once a month and enjoy the kind of familiarity that only comes from a shared history and deep trust.

It is comfortable and reassuring to spend time with someone who knows where you came from and is more interested in who you are than in what you've accomplished.

Our lunchtime conversations are always engaging, and I come away feeling energized and emotionally and intellectually enriched.

Do you have an old friend for whom you are grateful? Do you need to reconnect with someone from your past?

—SJP

March 6

I QUOTE THE LATE William Sloane Coffin: "Descartes had it wrong: 'Cognito ergo sum'? (I think, therefore I am). Nonsense. 'Amo, ergo sum.' (I love, therefore I am). There is no smaller package in the world than that of a person all wrapped up in himself."

Are you grateful today that you have been given the capacity to love, as well as people to love?

—JAA

March 7

BECAUSE OUR SON RONALD loves old movies, my wife and I watch them with him regularly. The more I watch, the more I realize that we never used to be exposed to car chases that end in massive explosions. We never saw heads blown off and blood flowing from wounds. Are the old movies unrealistic? Yes, I guess so, but the question is, "Do I need to see the blood and gore to know that someone has been shot or wounded?"

As a writer, I've been taught that everything should move a story forward in some way, so my other question is, "Does the hyper-realistic violence in today's films move the story forward?" I think not, but this is not a screed about violence in movies (though I could write such a screed). It's simply an observation about how filmmakers used to concentrate on stories in films, whereas now, in the great majority of them—not all, but the great majority—the directors substitute special effects for storytelling. I am grateful for the few good new films, the good stories, and the good acting. We just need more. Meanwhile, give me old movies with a good story, some civilized behavior, and good old-fashioned love scenes, and spare me the blood and guts.

Would you also be grateful for a little more love and a lot less violence?

—JAA

March 8

OUR FRIEND VIRGINIA TRAXLER is a doula, a woman who is with and supports women giving birth. In her book, *Birthing, An Act of Courage*, she writes about being present: "One important aspect of being a doula . . . is to be fully present with a woman wherever she is: in her pain, in her fear, in her confusion, in her despair, in her ecstasy. To be with her, not to change her, or make decisions for her or quiet her, but to give her a woman's hand, to wrap her in woman essence so that she knows and feels herself a birth giver, carrying life as it grows, unfolds and emerges into the world . . . ."

I am grateful for Virginia and the wonderful work she does.

Do you know someone who devotes herself or himself to helping others in critical periods of life? Be grateful today for that person.

—JAA

March 9

"Appreciation is a wonderful thing. It makes what is wonderful in others belong to us as well." (Voltaire)

I EXPERIENCE THIS FEELING whenever I'm with someone I admire, see a wonderful play, or hear a wonderful concert. My appreciation for the talents of others gives me a sense that I am sharing in who they are or what they do, and it fills me with gratitude. And it sometimes comes in unexpected places. A few years ago, I did a poetry class with "at risk" students in a local high school. Some of their poems were better than others, of course, but all of them represented honest effort to find their voices through poetry, and I found myself appreciating those young poets as much as the established poets I'd heard.

Do you recognize and appreciate the "wonderfulness" of others?

—JAA

March 10

EVERY TUESDAY AND THURSDAY, I attend an exercise class at a nearby fitness center. Usually six to eight women show up for an hour of aerobic and strength training, using weights, trampolines, medicine balls, and elastic bands.

I've been at this for half a dozen years now, and the class has become a valued fixture of my weekly routine. I protect these mornings from the encroachment of meetings, social engagements, or other distractions.

I know some of my classmates only by first names, yet these familiar faces seem like friends. Between panting and puffing, we chat about movies, children, weather, and an occasional current event.

Two years ago, a young woman with Down syndrome joined the class. At first, everyone was overly attentive, wanting to help her at every turn. But she was patient with us, and after a while, we all settled back into our normal routine.

She is no longer someone different, someone "special." She's just a woman trying to stay fit—and chatting about movies, weather, and sore muscles. I am grateful for her presence in the class. It's a healthier atmosphere for all of us.

Be grateful today for how our society now welcomes those it used to keep on the margins of daily life.

—SJP

March 11

IN THEIR BOOK, *Walk Out Walk On*, authors Margaret Wheatley and Deborah Frieze ask, "Why do we deny that humans need to celebrate?" Then they point out, "Cave paintings from thousands of years ago depict our ancestors dancing, not sitting in meetings."

Having sat in far more than my fair share of meetings over the years, this really hit home, and after reading it there was only one thing to do: I stood up and danced.

Why don't you stop reading this book right now and dance, and, if you can't physically dance, close your eyes and think about dancing?

—JAA

March 12

AFTER ALMOST FIFTY YEARS of smoking, my sister, Eve, has given up cigarettes.

I never imagined she would. Over the years, when family and friends urged her to quit, she stubbornly insisted that she had no intention of doing so. Nagging her about the health risks of tobacco only seemed to reinforce her insistence on lighting up when and if she liked.

But, for whatever reason, she decided one day to stop smoking. It hasn't been easy—especially when she lives with two other smokers.

But that same determination and willfulness on display when she ignored the pleas of anti-smokers is now a tremendous asset in her fight to quit.

It takes enormous strength and willpower every single day to give up the powerfully addictive tobacco habit. I am grateful that Eve has chosen to quit smoking and so proud of her stubborn determination!

Is someone you know battling addiction? Are you grateful for their resolve?

—SJP

March 13

THE THEOLOGIAN RABBI ABRAHAM Joshua Heschel said that the beginning of religious experience is to feel amazement at the world. And I don't think he was referring to the vastness of space or the (possible) existence of the Higgs boson particle (sometimes called the "God" particle) any more than he was thinking about the amazing journey from lowly caterpillar to glorious butterfly or the rebirth of the earth from winter into spring. If anyone wants to start on a spiritual journey toward God, he or she does not have to go far. The backyard will do just fine.

If you can feel amazed by the world and your place in it, then you are also feeling gratitude for the world and your place in it.

—JAA

March 14

I READ OBITUARIES, NOT because I'm morbid but because I'm interested in people's life stories. Everyone has a story, and everyone has interests and accomplishments. We pay a lot of attention to celebrities or well-known community leaders and their accomplishments, but in turning the newspaper pages to the obituary section where the stories of everyday people are told, I've been moved by the mosaic of acts large and small that together create the spiritual ebb and flow of the community. It is a great source of gratitude for me to know that I live in the midst of people who, in going about their daily lives, are also enriching a part of my life.

Can you identify, and are you grateful for the people in your community or club or church who help to enrich your life?

—JAA

March 15

"Now and then it's good to pause in our pursuit of happiness and just be happy." (Guillaume Apollinaire)

SOMEONE ONCE SAID THAT happiness is an inside job. Let me add that happiness is tantamount to gratitude, which is also an inside job. The person who is grateful need not worry about being happy, because gratitude flows from everything that inspires our happiness.

Be grateful for your happiness, and be happy for your gratitude.

—JAA

March 16

I HAVE BELONGED TO a book group for almost twenty-five years. There are now twelve of us, eight of whom have been part of the group since the first gathering.

Each month we meet for lunch at someone's house, and after eating we retire to the living room for discussion. The woman who chooses the book provides background on the author and leads the discussion. It usually takes only a few minutes before we break into chaos, all talking at once, interrupting one another or having side conversations. Somehow we manage to have fun and learn from one another despite the often free-for-all style of conversation.

Many of the books selected are ones I would never read on my own. Yet that is the beauty and value of a book club—being exposed to books you otherwise would have missed. I am grateful for that.

Over the years we have shared more than 200 books with one another, everything from biographies and historical novels to science fiction and spy mysteries. It is remarkable to have that much reading in common with friends. Surely it has shaped us in some small way and expanded our horizons. I know it has done so for me.

Be grateful if you are part of a social group that enriches your life.

—SJP

March 17

I HAVE INHERITED THE catalogue to my late brother's bathroom plunger collection. Yes, I mean plunger as in plumber's friend. He started the collection as a parody of all the "collectibles" that became so popular among his circle of friends. He'd visit a friend's home and immediately be shown a collection of, say, antique bottles or old roadside signs. It was after viewing a friend's collection of glass insulators, such as those once used on utility wires, that he decided to respond with his own collection. He chose bathroom plungers. After putting together a collection and displaying them along the wall of his home office, he developed a catalogue with a humorous story of the history of each one, all done with the utmost seriousness. I don't know what happened to the collection after his death, but I have a copy of the catalogue. It's very funny, and every once in a while, I find myself (*ahem*) plunging into it. And of course I'm grateful for it, and for the memories of my whimsical brother.

Is there someone who brings whimsy into your life? If not, try bringing a little whimsy into someone else's life.

—JAA

March 18

RAM DASS WROTE A wonderful book titled *How Can I Help?* In it, he speaks to all of us: "Caring is a reflex. Someone slips, your arm goes out. A car is in a ditch, you join others and push . . . .You live, you help . . . girding against the flood . . . setting up a community meeting . . . preparing a funeral . . . people seem to know their part. . . . Needs are anticipated, and glances of appreciation among us are enough to confirm that it's all going well."

Are there those who need and would be grateful for your help today?

—JAA

March 19

"Gratitude is the fairest blossom which springs from the soul; and the heart of man knoweth none more fragrant." (Hosea Ballou)

I AM A GARDENER and consider the life of plants as a metaphor for human life. In trying to put this thought into words, I find I can say it no better than the two quotes here. The following comment suggests that the blessings we count are our soul's gardeners:

"Gratitude is born in hearts that take time to count up past mercies. They are the charming gardeners who make our souls blossom." (Charles Edward Jefferson)

This is a good day to count your blessings and make your soul blossom.

—JAA

March 20

THE WORLD HAS BECOME so noisy these days that I am grateful when I go into a public place in which the people are having quiet conversations. Mark Twain expressed my opinion perfectly: "If animals could speak, the dog would be a blundering outspoken fellow; but the cat would have the rare grace of never saying a word too much." The challenge for me, of course, is to practice what I preach and not talk too much. That will probably make my family and friends grateful.

Be grateful for the gift of speech, and be grateful if you know when and when not to use it.

—JAA

March 21

I TALK ABOUT ALMOST everything with my hair stylist. She's a woman in her mid-forties with four children she has raised pretty much on her own. We both talk about our kids a lot. She has faced serious challenges over the years in rearing a now adult son and daughter and sixteen-year-old twin girls, but she has been remarkably successful by anybody's standards.

When I asked her about gratitude, she didn't hesitate: "When I look at my children, I am in awe of having the privilege of raising them, of just being worthy to have their lives entrusted to me. I feel really blessed to be a mother—their mother."

She spoke eloquently of something we don't always recognize—the power of motherhood or parenthood to bring out the best in us.

Today, ponder with gratitude the blessing of children and those in whose care they are nourished.

—SJP

March 22

IN LEADERSHIP CLASSES, I have often said that the six most useful words for any leader are these: "I could be wrong about that." Of course, those are useful words for all of us any time we have a disagreement, but too often we feel it's more important to insist on our viewpoint than ever to admit we might be wrong. When I finally realized that it was not weakness to admit mistakes, I felt liberated. I no longer felt required to defend my viewpoint against all arguments. And I became more grateful for the viewpoints of others.

Have you sometimes felt liberated by your willingness to listen to other ideas and viewpoints? If not, think about that today, and try it.

—JAA

March 23

MY DEAR FRIEND, BARBARA, sent me an e-mail the other day, saying, "Two things to be grateful for—raindrops and cameras." Attached was a slide show of exquisite photographs of raindrops on flowers and this explanation:

> When asked what is the most important invention in the last 200 years, a historian commented that the camera has got to be one of the most important inventions in the last 200 years, if not the most important. The oldest surviving permanent photograph of the image formed in a camera was created in 1826 or 1827 by the French inventor Joseph Nicéphore Niépce. The number of uses for a camera today are infinite, ranging from taking pictures of galaxies in far away space to submicroscopic photos with an electron microscope.

The attachment was just one of many collections of beautiful photographs that circulate on the Internet and are forwarded to millions of people for no other reason than to share their beauty.

I am grateful for the invention and refinement of cameras, for the development of the Internet, and for the human urge to share such beauty.

Consider with gratitude the pleasure that you derive from sharing photographs.

—SJP

March 24

I RECEIVED THESE WORDS today from an avid gardener friend: "I am grateful for the rare lagniappe day in March when the winds cease their blowing, the sun begins to warm the earth, and the weeds are easy to pull from their sanctuary under the leaves."

Are you grateful today for the weather, whatever it is?

—JAA

March 25

I HAVE ALWAYS TAKEN my sister for granted—but in a good way, if you know what I mean. I know that she is there for me, should I need her love and support. And I hope she takes me for granted in the same way.

But that kind of confidence in family ties can lead to neglect. And I confess that over the years I have become guilty of that very thing. So recently, I have made a conscious effort to renew and nurture my relationship with my sister. We have started getting together for coffee or lunch on a regular basis and finding that we have lots to talk about beyond family matters.

Of course, we have known each other our whole lives and seen one another through some truly difficult times, but we have never been the sort of sisters who are best friends.

Still, I am grateful for her, and I know I can count on her and she on me. And that is more than enough.

Do you need to rediscover and appreciate a family relationship?

—SJP

March 26

I HAD A FRIEND who used to insist that we invent our lives as we go along. That sounds too mechanical to me. I want to think that living life is an art and that the person who does it well is an artist, not an engineer. Of course, that's my prejudice as a writer. I read once that life is a canvas and that we should use all the paint we can in creating the painting that is our lives. In my case, I feel that I am writing my own story every day, and the challenge is to make it not only interesting but also useful and, if I do it well enough, inspiring. Part of creating the story of my life is trying to live in gratitude every day.

Whatever metaphor you use to think about your life—inventing, writing, or painting—be grateful for the opportunity today to make it beautiful and useful.

—JAA

March 27

"Be happy. Stay happy. Love your family and friends and forget the people who don't make sense." (author unknown)

AND WHO ARE THE people who don't make sense? I don't know your answer, but I think they are the people who seem to complain all the time. They never find anything right in the world. They're the people who seem to find some identity in criticizing how others do things, and of course they would be able to do those things better if only someone would give them the chance. There are lots of those people these days, and there's no way to persuade these incorrigible complainers to change, so don't spend your time trying. That would not make sense. Listen politely, if you have to, and then be happy, stay happy, and let gratitude fill the way you look at the world.

Be grateful today for the happy, loving people, and resolve to be one yourself.

—JAA

March 28

I'M NO PRUDE, but I find myself offended by the incessant profanity of what passes for humor these days. As a devotee of the first amendment, I accept the right of the so-called comedians to use whatever language they think will get a laugh, but when I hear a barrage of tasteless and just plain ugly words, I am grateful to Shakespeare for leaving a road map to the profound depths and beauty possible with the English language. Plus, he wrote a lot of funny, laugh-out-loud scenes, and he was no prude either.

Take time today to read a piece of good literature, and be grateful for the writers who can still use our language beautifully.

—JAA

March 29

MY LATE FATHER AND his brother, Uncle Elond, worked hard every day except Sunday. They did take a break from time to time, however, to play checkers. There was no checker set; rather, they used a piece of lumber about the size of a checkerboard and painted with the appropriate number and layout of squares. For checker pieces, they used Coca-Cola bottle caps, upside down and right-side up to designate whose piece was whose. That old piece of lumber, faded but still set up with the bottle caps ready for a game, sits in my office today. Behind it is a black and white photo of the two men, the checkerboard between them, studying their next moves. I am grateful for their memory and for the reminder that even the hardest work should be balanced by some pleasure and companionship.

Be grateful for your work today, but also be grateful for the times you put it aside and concentrate on fellowship and fun.

—JAA

March 30

"The question of bread for myself is a material question, but the question of bread for my neighbor is a spiritual question." (Nikolai Berdyaev)

OUR CHURCH AND ITS members are dependable supporters of homeless shelters for all kinds of people without homes or resources, from displaced families to struggling addicts to immigrants trying to make a start in America. I am grateful for this work and the compassion it evidences. I think it is just the kind of interest and activity with which a church should be involved, because the need is not just material but also spiritual.

Are you grateful for opportunities to think beyond your material needs to the material and spiritual needs of others?

—JAA

March 31

I'M TAKING THE BARBECUE grill out of storage today. The weather may still be a little cool, but I plan to fire up the grill and cook something this evening, even if I have to wear a coat and gloves. I say that with gratitude for the barbecue season soon to come.

Perhaps it's time for you to cook outdoors today. If so, be grateful for that. If not, be patient.

—JAA

April 1

LET'S START THIS MONTH by thinking about optimism as a virtue. Some people may ask how it is possible to be optimistic in a world so full of bad news. The answer is not only simple but also realistic: look for the good news. The truth is that there is more good news than bad news in this world, and while we can't discount the bad news, we need not dwell on it either. Optimism, like other virtues, is a way of being, thus it is one of the prerequisites of gratitude. We are grateful for what has been and what is, but we are also grateful for what is yet to be, which is the same as optimism.

Here's what others have said about optimism:

"A pessimist sees the difficulty in every opportunity; an optimist sees the opportunity in every difficulty." (Winston Churchill)

"Write it on your heart that every day is the best day in the year." (Ralph Waldo Emerson)

"Even the darkest night will end and the sun will rise." (Victor Hugo)

Look for the good news today, and be grateful for what is yet to be.

—JAA

April 2

MY FRIEND, DENISE, GETS absolutely jubilant about the arrival of spring. She says it is hard for her to put her excitement into words, but the change in seasons has a spiritual quality. "It starts with my dad's horses," she gushes. "The new grass begins popping up, and once again the horses have fresh food for grazing. The bulbs start sprouting and the trees bud out and the birds begin to sing. All of this is visible proof to me of God's promise to provide. Spring is the season that makes me feel God's presence in the very design of nature."

Today, let nature awaken in you a feeling of gratitude for life itself.

—SJP

April 3

IT'S EASY FOR MIDWESTERNERS to feel that the great places to live are someplace else—with mountains or oceans for recreation or urban centers for entertainment. But my friend Allison, a former Iowan who returns twice a year, shared her reaction with me during a recent visit. "When I arrived in Iowa, I quickly noticed how genuinely friendly everyone was," she explained. "No one was honking their horn, people were polite and smiling, it was just so refreshing and unlike L.A."

After she returned home, she followed up with this e-mail message, and I was reminded why I love living here: "When I think I am over-romanticizing how genuine and interesting and involved my Iowa friends are, a visit always confirms that they are even better than my rose-colored glasses version."

Do you need to be reminded to be grateful for the people and places in your life?

—SJP

April 4

I AM GRATEFUL FOR photographs. The other day, I realized once again just how much while cleaning out old files and coming across a treasure trove of snapshots taken through the years. I have to admit that I've not been good about organizing them and putting them in albums, yet, because I have not done that, I think I experienced a more intense sense of discovery by going through them willy-nilly. There were photos of everything and everyone you would expect, but for me it was like time travel, with this photo from 1984 and that one from 2010. The faces changed, sometimes looking older, and then, when I picked up a photo from an earlier year, the faces became young again.

Of course there were pictures of loved ones no longer living, but instead of feeling sad I was prompted to remember the good times when the photos were taken.

Thus the chore of cleaning out files became a blessing.

Surely you have photographs and memorabilia you should dig out and go through with gratitude for the memories.

—JAA

April 5

AFTER RETIREMENT, A FORMER colleague and his wife have placed service to others as a central focus of their lives. He explains it this way: "I'm a believer that somehow you get paid back for the money you give to the needy, but more so for the deeds you do and the mental support you give to others. Hopefully, this support . . . will help make the world a little smaller and more friendly." By sharing the fruits of their successful lives, my friends are expressing their gratitude in concrete ways.

In what concrete ways can you express your gratitude today?

—JAA

April 6

TOWARD THE END OF my son Jimmy's struggle with addiction, he wrote a moving poem that ended this way:

> Even while you think
> My God, how did all those years get by me,
> your face lifts up to the sky,
> breathing in, tasting
> this serene sacred gift.

And I am grateful for the sacred gift of Jimmy and his writings.

Have you lifted your eyes to the sky today, with gratitude for the serene sacred gift of life?

—JAA

April 7

"The weak can never forgive. Forgiveness is the attribute of the strong." (Mahatma Gandhi)

LIKE MANY PEOPLE, I have been conditioned to believe that some things are unforgiveable. When I consider a lot of the horrible, inhumane acts being committed in this world, I know it would take a morally stronger person than I to forgive them. But when it comes to the everyday transgressions of rudeness, personal betrayal, disloyalty, and even slander or attacks on my reputation, I can forgive those. Some would be more challenging than others, but I am committed to making forgiveness a part of the life of gratitude.

Consider today what, in the name of gratitude, you would be able to forgive.

—JAA

April 8

THE SURPRISE LILIES ARE pushing their foliage through the snow, as they have done every one of the thirty-eight years since I brought them to Iowa from my late mother's Mississippi garden. She called them "surprise lilies," though in Iowa most people call them "naked ladies." The foliage appears and becomes very lush, then dies back and disappears as if nothing were growing there. In August, when many flowers are fading in the heat and you've forgotten about the lilies, surprise, here they come: stalks of beautiful pink flowers. I'm always grateful for their late summer color.

Plant something or do something today that will bring you a gratitude surprise at just the right time.

—JAA

April 9

SEVERAL YEARS AGO, a friend who is an actress by training began volunteering in a woman's prison with the goal of helping the inmates gain a sense of self-esteem and confidence. She did this by staging theatrical productions starring the inmates. As in so many situations, those who help end up being those who are helped. Here is her response to the experience: "Surely God is everywhere in our world. But it is still more illuminating for me to feel God's presence inside the prison walls. I wonder if spirituality in captivity resonates more? Did the inmates in that prison cross my path to help me, or vice versa? Probably both, and for that I am grateful every day."

Have you sometimes found that in helping others you also are helped? It's a precious experience and worth your gratitude.

—JAA

April 10

MY SON JIMMY IS a talented musician who traveled regionally with a rock band. He is personable and charming. Throughout his life, everyone has liked Jimmy—except Jimmy. Whatever the reasons, he found his self-confidence through alcohol and drugs, both of which are occupational hazards of a rock musician's life on the road.

He has been dry and sober for four years, and today he and I leave on a long driving trip. We will go from home in Des Moines, Iowa, head south to St. Louis, and then travel along the Mississippi River to Memphis. After seeing family, we will go to the Rock 'n' Soul Museum in Memphis.

We will spend time with more family, and then we'll get on Highway 61, the famous blues highway that goes south through Delta country. At Clarksdale, we'll visit the Mississippi Delta Blues Museum. We'll stop for barbecue and sweetened iced tea and maybe throw some rocks in the Mighty Mississippi.

Then it's on to New Orleans and more museums, including the city's famous World War II museum. Jimmy is an expert on World War II, and I suspect we'll spend the better part of a day there.

Then it's more music, gumbo, oysters on the half shell, jambalaya, crawfish bisque, and po'boys.

New Orleans has one of the highest per capita rates of alcohol consumption in the country, but there'll be none for us.

After New Orleans, we head north to Arkansas, to Missouri, and finally home to Iowa. Am I grateful for the trip? It's not that; I'm simply grateful that Jimmy and I will be together for that length of time. I suspect we have a lot to talk about.

Is this a good day to plan a getaway with someone for whom you are grateful and with whom you need to spend some time?

—JAA

CHOOSING GRATITUDE

April 11

I AM SO GRATEFUL for my in-laws. I suppose that isn't such an astonishing thing to say, except that a lot of people seem to find much to criticize about their in-laws. Not me. When I was first welcomed into the family, they were so nice I figured I must be getting some kind of special treatment. It did not take long to realize that they are people who live their values to a high degree; they treat one another with the same loving kindness they showed me. To put it another way, what you see is what you get. They set what I think should be the standard for families. And after thirty-one years, I know beyond any doubt that it ain't phony. What a blessing for them all and, of course, for me.

We should all be grateful for our families, though I know many who are not. Are you?

—JAA

April 12

FAITH

When you come to the edge
of all the light you know,
And are about to step off
into the darkness of the unknown,
Faith is knowing
one of two things will happen:
There will be something solid to stand on,
or you will be taught how to fly.

           (Anonymous)

Think about this poem with gratitude today.

—JAA

April 13

GOETHE WROTE THAT IF we want to make life easy, we should make it hard. I had no idea what that meant when I first read it, but now I think it is about how we often make our lives hard when we don't have to. We turn small problems into big ones; we turn frustrations into crises; we turn disagreements into arguments. If we can stop reacting to life negatively and try being grateful for our lives—problems and all—then life becomes easy. When I feel frustrated and angry, I try to ask myself this question: "Why do I think my problems should be different from those of most of the other people in the world?" Then I focus on the fact that I have a choice; I can choose to make life hard or easy, depending on my attitude. That's what Goethe should have meant, even if he didn't.

Make today the day when you consciously make your life easier through the practice of gratitude.

—JAA

April 14

THE NEXT-DOOR NEIGHBORS' little daughter came over this morning to show us a picture she had painted. It reminded me of how neighborhoods evolve and change as families evolve and change. When we first moved here, there were young children everywhere, and the air was filled with their laugher and noisy play. Then some of them began to appear in uniforms of one sport or another. Then came skateboards, then loud cars, then wedding showers, and, suddenly it seemed, that generation was gone. In a few years, as the houses changed owners, young couples pushing strollers began to appear, along with young children accompanied by the laughter and noises of play. I am grateful to be part of this neighborhood and to be a witness to its ever-changing circle of life.

Are you grateful today for where you live and for all the life around you?

—JAA

April 15

"I like to pay taxes. With them, I buy civilization." (Oliver Wendell Holmes, Jr.)

WHEN MY WISE FATHER-IN-LAW hears people complain about how taxes suppress the incentive to succeed, he says, "You mean I should just stop trying to make money because that only means I have to pay taxes? The way I figure it, the more taxes I pay, the more money I've made."

I'm sure there will never be agreement on what the right amount of taxes should be, but I am sure of this: I have no complaints. I am grateful for all the benefits of living in this country, even with its warts and flaws. I absolutely agree with the late Justice Holmes.

Before you file your tax return today, list with gratitude all the benefits of living in the USA.

—JAA

April 16

"A good memory is one that can remember the day's blessings and forget the day's troubles."
"Prayers go up and blessings come down." (Yiddish proverbs)

HOW MANY PEOPLE do you know who, at the end of the workday, complain about all the bad things that are going on either in their workplace or in the world or both? It would be wonderful if they could attempt to live in gratitude, because gratitude is the very foundation of these proverbs.

Can you let go of today's troubles and develop a "good memory"?

—JAA

April 17

WITH ALL THE TALK about genetic engineering of plants these days, it's easy to forget the old-fashioned way that horticultural pioneers developed new plant varieties. I'm thinking specifically of a glorious dogwood tree and the azalea- and rhododendron-like beauties in my own yard. I say "like" because I don't know how they were developed. I grew up in the South, and for many years after I moved North, I missed the azaleas and dogwoods in the spring. My mother always reminded me of what I was missing by reporting when each plant was blooming, followed of course by the admonition to come visit. I now wish she were alive to see what the horticulturists have wrought for our cold climate. Believe me, I am grateful every spring for their good work.

Be grateful today for people whose work touches your life in ways you probably never think about.

—JAA

April 18

A WELL-KNOWN AFRICAN-AMERICAN SINGER spoke to a church group recently and told this story. In his growing-up years, he was frequently taunted and discriminated against socially at school. When he would go home and tell his mother about the hurtful words of the other kids, she would say, "You get down on your knees right now and pray for those folks."

I can't imagine anything more difficult to do than to pray for people whose despicable behavior has hurt you deeply. And yet the mother was teaching a powerful lesson in "turning the other cheek."

Be grateful when you have the courage to speak against injustice or when you are able to turn the other cheek yourself.

—JAA

April 19

EACH YEAR, A LOCAL counseling center holds a fundraising luncheon to help provide counseling for women and girls. The event is called Women Helping Women and, with the support of a hardworking committee and an inspirational speaker, draws several hundred attendees.

It strikes me that the name, Women Helping Women, is the perfect description for what they are trying to do. It's not called Us Helping Them, The Fortunate Helping the Unfortunate, The Healthy Helping the Sick, or The Rich Helping the Poor.

Women Helping Women brings to mind a circle—with women interlocking their arms and holding each other up. We all *need* help at times in our lives, and we are all able to *give* help at times in our lives.

Are you grateful for the relationships built through helping one another? Do you allow yourself to give and to receive help with grace?

—SJP

April 20

I USED TO DRIVE by an old country church that, even though it was in bad shape, still had the classic architecture envisioned by the Iowa immigrant farmers who built it in the mid-1800s. I felt it was a shame for it to deteriorate into a shell of itself and thought someone should try to save it. To make the story short, a friend and I contacted an architect who judged the structure to be sound and worth restoring. It could not be done as a church because its congregation had moved to town, so we restored it as a house. I no longer own it, but I still drive by every once in a while. The owners have done an addition much in keeping with the basic look. Someday I'll stop and express my gratitude to them.

Be grateful for old buildings and houses that remind you of the world as it used to be.

—JAA

April 21

EVERY YEAR AT EASTER, our church hosts a candlelit labyrinth walk. The labyrinth walk is drawn on a canvas that is rolled out on the floor. It is designed and structured in the style of the one built into the floor of the great cathedral in Chartres, France.

As the literature explains, "The labyrinth's path is like the path of life. There are twists and turns, feelings of being lost, encounters with others on your path, the thrill of accomplishment at the center, and sometimes a flash of insight before returning."

Unlike many church rituals and celebrations, this is not a practice with which I grew up. The very fact that it is outside my normal traditions gives it fresh power to bring new insights.

Are you open to new experiences that may nourish your spirit and open your heart? Be grateful for the twists and turns on your path.

—SJP

April 22

"It is one of the blessings of old friends that you can afford to be stupid with them." (Ralph Waldo Emerson)

I CAN'T SPEAK FOR women, but when men get together, particularly at some kind of reunion, we often take on the personalities we used to have, almost as if we were transported back in time. And let me be honest: we can become almost downright silly, saying and doing things we've not done in years and would not say or do in any other setting. I'm grateful that the wise Mr. Emerson has given us permission, and I am grateful for those good times and sweet memories.

Do you have friends with whom you can let yourself be a kid again?

—JAA

April 23

THE DAFFODILS ARE MAKING quite a show in our backyard, as they do every spring. These hardy flowers don't require anything of me, yet I feel some sort of motherly pride in their annual burst of color. I find myself excitedly inviting friends and neighbors to come by to see them in all their bright, hopeful beauty.

These encouraging harbingers of spring are universal symbols of new life. A small article in the newspaper reminded me of this the other day. It recounted the gift of a million bulbs that a Dutch millionaire, the city of Rotterdam, and other donors sent to New York City following the tragic deaths of 9-11. Volunteers planted the bulbs, and in the spring of 2002, glorious yellow daffodils appeared in every bare patch of earth across the city.

Even in the midst of tragic and evil acts, human kindness can break through. Put your faith in the human capacity for love, and be grateful for those who believe in beauty and hope.

—SJP

April 24

IN TALKING ABOUT HOW we Americans often approach our work, my minister David Ruhe once said, "It's not that we bite off more than we can chew; it's that we bite off more than we can savor." What that means to me is that we need to be able to get away from the drudgery of work and get into the joy of work.

There is much to write about the spirit of work, and three of the most important points are these: we should be grateful for work itself, we should be grateful for the people we work with, and we should be grateful for the grace of our spiritual possibilities at work.

Today, be grateful for the work you have chosen to do.

—JAA

April 25

THE INTENSE INTEREST IN a recent lottery jackpot over $300 million got me thinking about the reasons people are willing to spend their money to buy a 1 in 175 million chance to be a winner.

When you ask most people what they would do with the money if they won, they describe the luxuries they'd buy—a new home, a fancy car or boat, or an exotic vacation. And then invariably they add, "Then I'd set up a foundation to give some of the money to charities."

It seems to me that one of the things you buy with that lottery ticket is the opportunity to dream about what you have always wanted to do, and one of those dreams is to do something generous for others—to be a philanthropist.

That is a wonderful impulse—to do for others, to make a difference in the world through giving generously. But you don't have to win a jackpot to be a philanthropist. If every person who bought a lottery ticket gave that same amount to a church or charity, there would be millions more philanthropists and hundreds of millions more dollars in charitable donations.

If you dream of being generous, you needn't wait to win a jackpot. Do something that makes you feel generous today. You will be grateful you did.

—SJP

April 26

YEARS AGO, A FRIEND gave me an antique brass shoehorn, a special gift. I didn't use it for a while because I considered it a piece of art. Then one day I thought, "How in the world can using this thing damage it?" So I started using it, and now, every day when I put on my shoes, I think of my old friend with gratitude, not for the shoehorn but for the friendship.

Do you have useful reminders of beloved friends or family? Be grateful for those, and use them.

—JAA

April 27

I RECEIVED A GRATITUDE e-mail from a friend and former business colleague whom I have never thought of as particularly religious. He wrote, "I cannot believe how beautiful our spring is. It does take your breath away and is truly a faith renewer. This did not come to be by a simple neutron bumping into a couple of protons a zillion years ago." I was left to draw my own conclusion about how he thinks "this" came to be. I know what he meant, and so do you.

If you're having a beautiful spring day, express your gratitude, as my friend did, by saying how it did not come to be, or by saying how it did come to be.

—JAA

April 28

IN A PREVIOUS BOOK, I wrote about the gratitude walk, which is the way I try to start each day, weather permitting. It's really more than a walk; it's a meditation and a spiritual discipline. The objective is to clear my mind of all the worries of life and the world and simply to gaze with gratitude on whatever I see: parents pushing strollers, squirrels playing in the trees or scolding my cat, neighbor children playing or heading to school. I may be grateful for the way the sun hits the trees on our street or the aroma of a just-mowed lawn—or, in winter, the sparkle of frosting on the trees. Looked at with gratitude, it's all beautiful.

Try a gratitude walk today, and see if it doesn't lift your spirits.

—JAA

April 29

A FRIEND SHARED THESE lines from a poem I'd not read before:

Sweet is the breath of vernal shower,
The bee's collected treasures sweet,
Sweet music's melting fall, but sweeter yet
The still small voice of gratitude.
(From *Ode for Music* by Thomas Gray)

Are you listening today for the still, small voice of gratitude?

—JAA

April 30

THE GEESE ARE MOVING north again, long V-shaped strings of them. As a former fighter pilot, I can't resist stopping what I'm doing and looking up. They are such good flyers, not to mention navigators. And I love the story of how they help one another. They make a lot of sounds while they fly, and I've heard that the geese farther back in the formation are calling encouragement to the leader. Also, in the best contemporary sense of shared organizational responsibility, they shift positions, taking turns as leader. If we pay attention, we can learn some lessons from those high flyers.

Are you grateful for the people in the organizations you serve—and how you work to help each other?

—JAA

May 1

MORE THAN ANYTHING ELSE, respect means that every person must be treated as a person and not as a thing. This may be the most difficult virtue to maintain, because it means we have to treat even the people we don't like as fellow human beings. I've seen many examples, as perhaps you have, of people who profess to care for one another but who treat one another rudely. I've seen it at universities, in clubs, and even in churches. I think the best way to find respect for others is to look for the Divine in them, to find God in them, and, if we can't do that, then at least engage them with the assumption of good will between us.

If we are committed to living in gratitude, the commitment to respect others must be part of our very being.

Read now what others have written about respect:

"When you are content to be simply yourself and don't compare or compete, everybody will respect you." (Lao Tzu)

"I have no right, by anything I do or say, to demean a human being in his own eyes. What matters is not what I think of him; it is what he thinks of himself. To undermine a man's self-respect is a sin." (Antoine de Saint-Exupery)

"A youth is to be regarded with respect. How do you know that his future will not be equal to our present?" (Confucius)

"I speak to everyone in the same way, whether he is the garbage man or the president of the university." (Albert Einstein)

Identify someone today who you think does not respect you or whom you have trouble respecting. Then write down one step you can take to encourage mutual respect. If you don't succeed, you can be grateful that you tried.

—JAA

May 2

ALMOST EXACTLY ONE YEAR AGO, my husband and I were surprised and delighted when a young mother and her daughter from next door walked up our driveway pulling a red wagon. They rang our doorbell and handed us a May Day basket. We hadn't received one in years, but they haven't changed. The basket was made of a piece of construction paper twisted into a cone with a handle attached. It was filled with popcorn and a few candy kisses and some small purple violets.

All of it reminded me not only of making and delivering May Day baskets with my son in my early years of motherhood but also of the construction paper May Day baskets of my own childhood. This simple tradition may be one of the few rituals that have not been taken over by commercial interests. And because no one is advertising the occasion, the gift baskets come as an unexpected surprise.

This day can be like any other day, or, if you approach it with gratitude, you may just see it as an unanticipated gift.

—SJP

May 3

REINHOLD NIEBUHR, THE GREAT American theologian, wrote, "Love is rejoicing . . . in the otherness of the other." Thinking of my son Ronald's autism in the context of this quote, I offer this addendum: "Love is rejoicing in the differentness of the other." And I do, and I'm grateful for that.

Do you love someone whom other people may think of as "different"? Aren't you grateful that you've been given that person to love?

—JAA

May 4

A FEW YEARS AGO, some visionary leaders in my hometown decided to purchase the rundown building on Main Street that at one time housed the movie theater. Their dream was to restore it to its former purpose and create a vibrant community-gathering place.

The town hadn't had a movie house since the Palace Theater closed its doors decades before. The new theater would provide a modern screen and equipment for showing films and a stage for live performances by the local community theater group. The decision was made to form a nonprofit and solicit government grants and private donations. Volunteers put together a fund-raising plan and engaged an architect.

Many in town thought the project was too ambitious and that the goal would never be reached. Fortunately, the naysayers were wrong. Grants were obtained, and hundreds of people made donations both large and small. The Palace Theater was restored and reopened in less than a year.

Rehabbing the building was an important achievement, but even more important was the community spirit that developed as a result of sharing a common vision. The town's people felt good about themselves and what they had accomplished, and they were grateful for the sense of new possibilities ahead.

Do you embrace the opportunity to be part of a vision larger than yourself? Be grateful for those who dream big dreams.

—SJP

May 5

"To be able to look back on one's past life with satisfaction is to live twice."
(Martial)

NOT ONLY THAT, BUT it is to recognize with gratitude the people, places, and experiences that make up the essence of life's satisfactions. This is not to say that we should dwell in the past; only that we should appreciate all that has made us who we are and has put us on the road to the next source of life's satisfaction, whatever it may be.

Can you look back with gratitude for all of your life's satisfactions—and ahead to the satisfactions yet to come?

—JAA

May 6

"Twenty years from now, you will be more disappointed by the things you didn't do than by the ones you did." (Mark Twain)

ALTHOUGH I KNOW THAT it is a great waste to live in regret, I nonetheless look back at things I should have done and did not do, both personal and professional. The challenge is to turn those thoughts into lessons about how to live now. If I look back at all, I try to do it with gratitude for the things I did do.

Do you live with disappointment about the things you failed to do? Today, turn that disappointment into gratitude for what you were able to do.

—JAA

May 7

TEN YEARS AGO, OUR church built a large addition that included much needed space for classrooms, meetings, and community events. Part of the new construction was a coffee shop equipped with fancy espresso and cappuccino machines. It operated for a few years, but then it closed.

Two years ago, it reopened with a new purpose. The coffee shop now operates in partnership with a local high school that serves students with disabilities. The shop is open five days a week and staffed by students and volunteers. The students are gaining important employment skills, and the coffee shop is providing a community service. Those who volunteer find the experience rewarding and have learned a lot in the process.

One of the volunteers, a retired businessman, said, "These kids have very different lives from what I have; they face different challenges than others their age. I like being able to help them learn skills that will enable them to get a job. I've made lasting friendships with these young people, and that has truly been a blessing."

Express your gratitude to those who help others by volunteering their time and talents. Do you have gifts that you can share?

—SJP

May 8

CHRISTINA ROSSETTI WROTE THAT it is better by far that we should forget and smile than that we should remember and be sad.

Can you smile with gratitude even for things that are too painful to remember?

—JAA

May 9

A FEW YEARS AGO, I had the great privilege of meeting Sir Laurens van der Post. Of the many things I could say about him, one of the most impressive is this: even though he was a World War II prisoner of the Japanese, he was a leading voice for forgiveness of enemies after the war.

He once wrote,

> I have felt all my life that the individual must not wait for governments and he must not wait for groups and powerful people to do something. He must take care of what is on his doorstep; that is the material that he has in life and he must work with that. You do what is necessary at a given moment with all your heart and all your soul. You do not wait and say, well, there will be something better tomorrow. You do it, you accept it . . . .

How can you accept with gratitude the challenges on your own doorstep?

—JAA

May 10

"All the blessings we enjoy are Divine deposits, committed to our trust on this condition, that they should be dispensed for the benefit of our neighbors." (John Calvin)

I HAVE A FRIEND who refers to some of his neighbors and colleagues as "trust-funders," meaning that they have inherited a trust fund that allows them a level of material comfort for the rest of their lives. When I came across this quote, I thought, we're all trust-funders, and if we share those blessings, we will have a level of spiritual comfort for the rest of our lives. Now that's something to be grateful for.

Today, do a review of your own spiritual trust fund.

—JAA

May 11

IN MY EXPERIENCE, FORGIVENESS does not come easily, whether we are trying to forgive someone whom we feel has harmed or betrayed us, or we are trying to forgive ourselves for acts that harmed others.

I think true forgiveness requires more than is humanly possible, because genuine forgiveness is illogical, and, in a sense, it must ignore what is just. An eye for an eye makes sense; turning the other cheek does not.

That is why I think real forgiveness requires something outside the human norm—grace. Something must enter the equation that will allow us to stop thinking in terms of justice, or even mercy, but will eliminate the need for either: that something is called "grace." Perhaps the only way to forgive others or to forgive ourselves is to invite grace into our hearts and then wait for it to come.

Are you struggling with forgiveness? Set aside your mind's ledger and forget about what is just. Be grateful that grace trumps justice.

—SJP

May 12

"In ordinary life we hardly realize that we receive a great deal more than we give, and that it is only with gratitude that life becomes rich. It is very easy to overestimate the importance of our own achievements in comparison with what we owe others." (Dietrich Bonhoeffer)

LIKE MOST YOUNG MEN in America, I grew up with the myth of the self-made man. But my years in business taught me that no one makes it on his own; some of us just don't recognize the boosts we get along the way—which means we never develop gratitude for those helping hands.

Are you grateful today for those who have helped you along the way?

—JAA

May 13

I SOMETIMES REFER TO myself as a "half mystic" because I am drawn to what some call synchronicity and others call coincidence. There have been too many unexplained and unexplainable incidents or episodes in my life for me to write them off as "just one of those things." And they have happened throughout my life. My divorced mother once woke me in the middle of the night and said, "Call your father." I didn't do it, but I found out the next day that he had been rushed to the doctor—just in time, it turned out, to save his life.

A few years ago, I was in Atlanta on business and decided to visit the memorial garden where my late beloved sister-in-law Susie's ashes are scattered. As I was walking meditatively through the azaleas and pines, I heard Susie's voice. "Jimmy," she called, "are you here?" It was a surreal and somewhat frightening experience.

I hurried around the next bend and saw a woman, Susie's best friend. Her voice sounded exactly like Susie's. She ran to me and we hugged. After a moment, she said, "Jimmy, I dreamed about Susie last night. She appeared and said, 'I am still with you.' This morning I felt a very strong pull to visit this place. When I saw your name on the registry, it made the shiver. I guess you and I were supposed to be here today."

I guess so too. I felt so much gratitude for that "synchronicity" or "coincidence" or mystical connection, almost like being with Susie again.

Have you had such mystical experiences for which you are grateful?

—JAA

May 14

WOMEN HAVE AN ESPECIALLY difficult time balancing work and family obligations. Sometimes that is made worse by the expectations of children. When I first decided to run for public office after several years at home dedicated to childrearing, my son wasn't happy with me and let me know about it. He said to anyone who would listen, "I don't want my mom to be lieutenant governor; I just want her to be my mom."

It's human nature to want to hold on to the attention of those who love and care for us—and children naturally think of their own needs first. So it took several patient family conversations to convince Ronald that I would always be his mom regardless of what other work I did. And that together, Dad and I would be sure he had the care he needed.

That's why I treasure the note he wrote me a few months after I took office.

Happy Mother's Day
I love you Mom. I'm proud of your work.
Love,
Ronald

Have you had moments when you have been moved to gratitude by the encouragement and support of your loved ones?

—SJP

May 15

ON THE DAY BEFORE my mother's funeral, I visited the cemetery and found a man digging my mother's grave by hand, with a shovel. Days later, in gratitude, I wrote this poem:

Grave Digger
His name is Otis Cox
and the graves he digs with a spade are acts of love.
The red clay holds like concrete
still he makes it give up a place
for rich caskets and poor
working with sweat and sand
in the springing tightness of his hair
saying that machine digging
don't seem right if you know the dead person.
His pauses are slow as the digging
a foot always on the shovel.
Shaking a sad and wet face
drying his sorrow with a dust-orange white handkerchief
he delivers a eulogy:
"Miz Ruth always gimme a dipper of water."
Then among quail calls and Blackeyed Susans
Otis Cox shapes with grunt and sweat and shovel
a perfect work
a mystical place
a last connection with the living hand.
(from *Nights Under a Tin Roof*, 1983)

Let's be grateful today for the unnamed people who work quietly and without recognition to bring dignity to the burial of others.

—JAA

May 16

RAISING CHILDREN CAN BE a real challenge—and often children with disabilities stretch parents' limits.

During the early years of Ronald's life, I felt that I was not a good mother, that I should know how to do the right things to help Ronald with his autism, and that since I didn't, there was something wrong with me.

Sometimes, my goal was to just get through the day, hoping that tomorrow Ronald would be older and maybe capable of more than today. Things were not going well, and I was not feeling good about myself or about Ronald's future. I was normally an optimistic person, but I couldn't muster that optimism then.

Then something happened. I remember the moment clearly. I was in my living room feeling sad and helpless. I remember thinking this is too much for me. I am not equipped to raise this child. I am not smart enough, patient enough, strong enough, or loving enough. I simply can't do this alone.

I was ready to give up—to surrender!

And then it dawned on me. Of course I couldn't do this alone. Nobody could. But then, I didn't need to. There were so many people ready to help and so many people already helping.

Perhaps that doesn't seem profound to you, but it was to me. It was a revelation in the true meaning of the word.

If God is love—and I believe God is manifested through love—then God had been helping from the beginning and would go right on helping Ronald throughout his life. This weighty responsibility was not in my hands alone, and it never had been.

Be grateful for the many ways God's love is manifested through others in your life.

—SJP

May 17

IT'S THAT TIME OF year again when, throughout our city, people are turning their backyards and patios and driveways and garages into party rooms to celebrate someone's graduation. I'm grateful for this joyful hoopla because it is an important ritual. And every graduation leads to something. When I was young, I was encouraged to stay in school and get my "high school diploma," but by the time I entered high school, all the emphasis was on going to college. As I write this, my grandson has just graduated from college and is entering a program leading to a PhD in applied mathematics; his younger brother has graduated from high school and is off to study biology. So there are even more graduation parties in my future, and, believe me, that's something to anticipate and to be grateful for.

Do you have graduates for whom you are grateful? If so, celebrate their accomplishments this spring.

—JAA

May 18

MY FRIEND BILLIE MAGUIRE shared a story in which a large steamer set out from New York harbor. They were only a few miles from shore when a storm hit. An important passenger made his way to the bridge and urgently demanded that the captain return to shore. Finally the captain said to the passenger, "You are on a ship at sea. That means you're always just coming out of a storm, getting ready for a storm, or going through a storm. If you don't intend to cross the sea, you should never have taken the ship."

Of course, the story is about the journey of life and what we set ourselves to do. And Billie added this, in the words of Maya Angelou, "Wouldn't take nothing for my journey now!"

Are you grateful today for your life's journey, no matter how stormy it has been?

—JAA

May 19

A FRIEND SENT ME a story from the *LA Times* that she thought was a wonderful example of gratitude. The article tells of a young immigrant high school student with exceptional grades and aspirations to be an architect, but without financial resources to attend college and no ability to secure loans.

The student's former eighth-grade teacher, a single woman of modest means, has volunteered to pay for the student's college education. As the story explains, the teacher's own immigrant father worked sixteen-hour days, seven days a week, to put her through college. Her father is no longer living, so she has decided that this is how she can pay forward the gratitude she feels for her father's sacrifices. Her generosity is opening a door to a new world for this student.

Let the gratitude you feel for the gifts you have received express itself in generosity to others.

—SJP

May 20

"He who is not contented with what he has, would not be contented with what he would like to have." (Socrates)

SOMETIMES I THINK THE slogan of our consumer society is, "More, Bigger, Better!" I am not against people wanting to better themselves or better their situations, but I know what its like to convince myself that I need something I really don't need rather than living in gratitude for what I have.

Are you grateful for what you have rather than wanting what you don't have?

—JAA

May 21

MY MOTHER ALWAYS HAD the same response when one of her five children woke up complaining that he or she was ill and couldn't go to school.

Mom would say, "Get up, get dressed, and if you still don't feel well, you can go back to bed."

Somehow, once you were dressed and ready for school, you never felt bad enough to undress and climb back into bed. It was easier just to go to school.

I used that same strategy with my child, as I suspect my siblings did with theirs. It has served me pretty well in my own life too, whether getting myself up and dressed to go to the office or getting prepped and ready to start a new project.

My mother was one wise woman.

What important lessons did your mother teach you? Have you shared (with her) your gratitude for her wisdom?

—SJP

May 22

A FRIEND RECENTLY TOLD me about a time in which he faced the worst crisis of his life. He said a good friend told him that, despite his present pain and confusion, he would one day look back on that particular year with gratitude. He said he eventually did just that, and then he added, "Since then I've told myself that the best time to be alive is right now, because it's the only time I am alive."

And that is reason enough for all of us to be grateful.

Are you grateful for "now"—this minute, this hour, this day—as the best time to be alive?

—JAA

May 23

IN 1845, JAMES LOWELL wrote, "New occasions teach new duties, time makes ancient good uncouth." I love that line and particularly that choice of words. I also love its insistence that the idea of "good" must yield to new definitions and circumstances, that words like "good" and "truth" evolve. And I know this to be true. I grew up in the South, went to segregated schools, and saw African Americans subjected to insult and humiliation. In its time, in that place, that kind of treatment was the "truth" of racial relationships and was considered "good" for the social order. I am grateful for the courage of leaders, both black and white, who made new occasions for new duties and who defined that old "good" as uncouth, then risked much to bring about change.

Are there leaders in your community, church, state, or the nation to whom you are grateful for their moral commitment?

—JAA

May 24

FORTY YEARS AGO, MY beloved cousin Douglas Autry gave me some tomato seeds. "They make slowly, but they're worth the wait," he said. "They're kind of rough looking, but the taste is just like the old-fashioned tomatoes you remember."

Douglas died over a decade ago, and I still grow those tomatoes every year. I save seeds, dry them, and then put them in the freezer until the following spring. I've kept every year's seeds, and last year, believe it or not, I planted some seeds from the original batch Douglas gave me—and they sprouted and grew.

Eating those tomatoes was almost like communion with Douglas.

What growing and delicious things are you grateful for today?

—JAA

May 25

"Enough is a feast." (Buddhist proverb)

WHEN I GRADUATED FROM college, my ambition was to be a newspaperman and make fifty dollars a week. I thought that would be enough. As I progressed in my career and had a family, the concept of "enough" always seem to change, to the point it seemed I never had enough. I was not alone; almost everyone I knew was in the same rut: get a raise, make more, spend more, "need" more. I now realize that the problem lay in my definition of "enough." I am grateful that, twenty-five years ago, I expanded the definition of enough to focus on the people and relationships in my life instead of on money and material goods. When I did that, it became apparent that, indeed, enough is a feast.

How do you define enough; is it a feast or a never-ending struggle? Be grateful for everything in your life, and know it is enough.

—JAA

May 26

MOST OF THE SUCCESS I've achieved in life is testimony not so much to me as to the people who have taught and supported me along the way. I am grateful to family and friends, of course, but I am also the beneficiary of the dedication, hard work, and often compassion of teachers, particularly those who modeled and taught values. Carl Jung said that "an understanding heart is everything in a teacher." He said that we "look back with appreciation to the brilliant teachers, but with gratitude to those who touched our human feeling."

Have you had teachers who touched your human feeling? Breathe a prayer of gratitude for them today.

—JAA

May 27

I USED TO THINK that people who treated their dogs like family were a little silly. I like pets and have almost always had a cat or dog or both. But it wasn't until my son got a corgi that I became a little silly myself.

My husband and I now refer to Gilda as our "grand-dog." There's not much I won't do for this animal. Perhaps it is because she is such an important friend and companion for our son, Ronald.

When Jim, Ronald, and I make the two-hour drive to spend a weekend with my parents, we always take Gilda with us. (You can't justify leaving your "grand-dog" at a kennel unless it is absolutely necessary!)

At first I wasn't sure how my parents would react to having this pet around. My dad had never showed much affection for the family pets when we were growing up, and his general attitude was that animals should be treated like animals.

On one such visit to my parents' home last summer, Gilda was tied up outside while we all enjoyed a lunch my mom had prepared. When we got up from the table, my dad noted that it was hot out and asked if Gilda needed water. I began looking for an old plastic container to use for a dish, when, to my amazement, Dad pulled a cereal bowl from the cupboard, filled it with water, and took it out to Gilda. When I suggested that Mom might not want Gilda drinking from the family tableware, he said, "Don't worry, it's *my* oatmeal bowl."

Later, as we piled into the car to head home, Dad made a parting comment about his "great-grand-dog" as he waved good-bye. I couldn't help smiling.

How do you express your silly affection for someone or some living creature?

—SJP

May 28

IF OUR TASK IN life is, as Leo Tolstoy suggested, to become an increasingly better person, then I believe the first step is to live every day in gratitude. I'm not sure exactly how to know that I am becoming a better person, but if I remind myself to be grateful for this day whatever it brings, I'm on the right track. Another step is to identify a virtue I'm not so good at and then concentrate on it today. Does this take a lot of commitment? You bet. Am I able to do it every day? No. It is worth a try? Absolutely!

Be grateful today for yet another opportunity to be a better person.

—JAA

May 29

"I don't know what your destiny will be but one thing I know: the only ones among you who will be really happy are those who have sought and found how to serve." (Albert Schweitzer)

ONE OF THE MOST important revelations I've ever had was the discovery that an attitude of service is the twin of an attitude of gratitude. The best business leaders focus on serving their employees rather than bossing them. The best neighbors are always there with a helping hand. The best salespeople don't differentiate between big customers and small customers but serve all equally. And this kind of service goes beyond occasional helping to encompass a constant and reliable sensitivity to those who need to be served.

Is there a way today for you to serve someone who needs it?

—JAA

May 30

Higher Ground
My heart has no desire to stay
Where doubts arise and fears dismay;
Though some may dwell where these abound,
My prayer, my aim is higher ground.

I'VE ALWAYS LOVED THIS verse of the old hymn because it speaks to the determination to rise above the doubts and fears in life and keep moving onward and upward.

Be grateful today for the chance to always move spiritually onward and upward.

—JAA

May 31

I ONCE EXPRESSED SURPRISE to a friend who makes everyday use of her sterling silver flatware. "I learned that from my maternal grand-mother," she said, "who told me to always use the best you have for family and not just for the benefit of company. I will always be grateful for my grandmother's advice to treat the family like honored guests." It struck me that the advice is not just for tableware. We should show gratitude for our families every day by treating them like honored guests.

Make the extra effort today to show your family how grateful you are for them and that they are as important as any honored guest.

—JAA

June 1

SOMETIMES IT TAKES COURAGE just to get up in the morning and face the day. Sometimes it takes courage to express gratitude in a world in which so many things seem to go wrong. But without courage, we can never look beyond what's wrong and find gratitude for what's right in our lives. And part of what's right is demonstrated every day by the courage of those of us who face serious personal problems yet still find gratitude.

Read these writings about courage:

"Each time we face our fear, we gain strength, courage, and confidence in the doing." (Anonymous)

"To live, we must conquer incessantly, we must have the courage to be happy." (Henri Frederic Amiel)

"Keep your fears to yourself, but share your courage with others." (Robert Louis Stevenson)

"Courage is resistance to fear, mastery of fear—not absence of fear." (Mark Twain)

Write down any situations or challenges in your life that require courage to face, and be grateful that you are blessed with the courage to do so.

—JAA

June 2

As I WALK BY THE rosemary in the ceramic pot by the back door, I run my hands through the branches and bring the fragrance into the house with me. The aroma lingers for some time and reminds me of summer herbal gardens and outdoor grilling.

My husband has kept this plant alive for decades, nurturing it through the winter in his greenhouse. It's an effort lugging the heavy pot into a wheelbarrow, pushing it up the driveway, and lifting it into place on a shelf in the glass-covered enclosure—then reversing the process in the spring. If keeping plants over from year to year were up to me, I doubt that I would take the time and trouble. Therefore, I truly appreciate that he does. Year in and year out, that lovely shrub of rosemary greets friends who enter our backdoor with a perfume just there for the taking.

Our sense of smell can enhance our pleasure and enjoyment of the world around us. Be grateful for sensual pleasures, and, today, indulge in the simple delights of smell.

—SJP

June 3

ONE OF THE QUOTES I use most often in my leadership workshops is said to have hung on Albert Einstein's office wall: "Not everything that counts can be counted, and not everything that can be counted counts."

We have our stuff that can be counted. And we have our loved ones that can be counted.

Which of those really count?

Be grateful today for what really counts in life.

—JAA

June 4

ONCE BENEATH THE WILLOW
where the light played against your skin
and the taste of strawberries was still
on your lips as I kissed you, how I thought
everything would last forever!
If I was wrong, it was not for lack of love,
drawn gossamer against a terrifying age.
So gently the wind played in your hair;
so small a thing to have touched me
across those years, touches me still.
(A poem of memory by Phil Hey, used by permission)

For what sweet memories are you grateful today?

—JAA

June 5

I HAVE AN ELDERLY friend who, like many of his generation, has developed health problems that deprive him of his mobility. He was a medical corpsman in World War II assigned to the marines, and he made numerous combat landings in the South Pacific. In other words, he paid some demanding dues. Now, his wife expresses her gratitude to the Veterans Administration for sending an aide for two hours, Monday through Friday, to help my friend remain comfortably at home.

Do you have military veteran friends or relatives for whom you are grateful? Give them a call or drop them a line today.

—JAA

June 6

MY SON AND I just returned from a driving trip during which we visited the excellent World War II museum in New Orleans. It is an experience that changes the perception of that war from an abstraction into a terrible life-and-death reality. After all these years, we still owe a huge debt of gratitude for the sacrifices those men and women made.

Take a few minutes on this D-Day and breathe a prayer of gratitude for those who made it possible for us to freely breathe a prayer.

—JAA

June 7

MADRAP*
This is a place of daily miracles
where strangers sit in circles
and discover the lost language of love,
putting themselves back together,
fitting tears and anger and pain
like puzzle pieces
until their stories make sense again.
(from *Life after Mississippi*)

*Mercy Alcohol and Drug Rehabilitation Program

Are there therapies or programs that have helped one of your friends or loved ones? Spend a few minutes in gratitude for them today.

—JAA

June 8

"Remember this, that very little is needed to make a happy life." (Marcus Aurelius)

THIS QUOTE REMINDS ME of my grandmother. She was always happy, though it could have just seemed that way because she was always happy to see me. She had difficult times in her life, but she lived in gratitude. She was full of all the old sayings like, "Count your blessings every day," "If you have your health you have everything," and "Always help anyone in your family who needs help." She grew roses, and I was told that, during the Depression, she would stand in her rose garden every Sunday morning and pin rosebuds on the lapels of the young men on their way to church. I think it must have been one of the ways she expressed her gratitude.

Who in your family has blessed you through his or her words and actions? How can you show that person how grateful you are?

—JAA

June 9

"Now, let us acknowledge the wonder of our physical incarnation—that we are here, in these particular bodies, at these particular times, in these particular circumstances. May we never take for granted the gift of our individuality." (Saint Augustine of Hippo)

IN A COUNTRY PREOCCUPIED with physical appearances, I am grateful for this reminder that we ourselves, "in these particular bodies," are among the wonders of the world.

Take time today just to look in the mirror and be grateful for the wonder of yourself.

—JAA

June 10

MY HUSBAND AND I were surprised and pleased that our son Ronald was included in an invitation to the wedding of our friend's daughter. Still, we approached the event with some apprehension since, due to his autism, Ronald's behavior in social settings is sometimes unpredictable. The beautiful ceremony was held at a fine old Washington D.C. hotel, with dinner and dancing afterward. As the evening wore on, Ronald became more animated and decided to join the crowd on the dance floor.

I looked up at one point to see him dancing flamboyantly with the mother of the bride. Concerned that Ronald was monopolizing her attention, I decided to rescue her. But when I tried to free her from his exuberant embrace, my friend stopped me in my tracks. She politely but firmly informed me that she was having fun and so was he, and I needn't interrupt.

I found myself simultaneously feeling ashamed and grateful. I realized my concern about Ronald's behavior was based in part on my own embarrassment over his "differentness," and I was grateful for my friend's genuine acceptance of Ronald just as he is.

Are you grateful for the people in your life who love and accept you and yours without judgment?

—SJP

June 11

HERE IS A PROFOUND message from my friend, poet Betty Sue Flowers:

Hope
It's the part of the worm that wiggles
when the rest is around the hook.

Let that be a lesson for all of us, with gratitude for life's indomitable spirit.

—JAA

June 12

I OPENED AN E-MAIL recently that read, "Before you know, it will be time to suck da heads and squeeze da tips once again here in Pawleys Island!" It was an invitation from dear friend and co-author Peter Roy and his wife, Gillian. Peter is originally from New Orleans, and every year he hosts a big crawfish boil at his home. It is a joyful, multi-day event, a celebration of tradition, of heritage, of friendship, and of life. I am grateful for the Roys' commitment to keep it going year after year.

Are there ongoing rituals or celebrations for which you are grateful?

—JAA

June 13

I HAVE THE GOOD fortune to be married to a poet. Our library shelves are thick with poetry books, and over the years my husband has introduced me to many nationally famous poets and their work. Sometimes on a quiet evening, my husband and I settle in with a glass of wine while he reads from some new book by a well-known poet or a recently discovered one. To my great joy, I sometimes receive a beautiful verse from Jim tenderly composed for a special anniversary.

I doubt that I would have been exposed to so much poetry had I not been married to a poet. His favorite poets often become mine. One such is Mary Oliver. Her poem "The Summer Day" has a line I am fond of quoting: "What is it you plan to do with your one wild and precious life?" It is a question each of us must ponder for ourselves. Yet I can't help reflecting on the gratitude I feel that my husband has chosen to spend at least a portion of his "wild and precious life" as a poet. That choice has certainly enriched my life and the lives of so many others.

Read some poetry today, and be grateful for the wisdom of the poets and the beauty and richness of their art.

—SJP

June 14

PERHAPS BEING THE PARENT of a child with a disability has sensitized me, but I am persuaded that all the bad stuff in this world is being offset every day by the simple goodness of average people. For instance, a few days ago I was behind a young man with a mental disability in line at the supermarket. When the cashier, an attractive young woman, rang the total, $10.86, he handed her a ten-dollar bill. "Ten eighty-six," she said. The young man looked confused, then said, "I have ten dollars." The cashier smiled. "Okay," she said, then reached under the counter and pulled out her purse. "I have a dollar," she said. I was amazed.

The young man seemed not to know what had transpired, but he took his groceries and left.

"Do you know him?" I asked the cashier.

"No," she said. "I just see him in here every once in a while."

"Well, that was a generous and supportive thing you did." I tried to reimburse her.

She shrugged. "Everyone runs short of change sometimes."

Think about that a minute. The cashier herself was probably being paid eight dollars or so an hour, yet she was about to give her own money to help this young man out of an embarrassing and confusing situation.

When you recognize the innate goodness in someone, be grateful for that person's influence in this world.

—JAA

June 15

MY SON JIMMY HAS a great sense of humor, and sometimes it has a bit of an edge to it. Take for instance this note in a Father's Day card: "Thank God for you. And I do. You are at the top of my gratitude list. I worship the very quicksand you walk upon."

There's more insight in that last sentence than you might think.

Have you had messages with private meanings for which you are grateful?
—JAA

June 16

EVERYONE HAS A STORY. Not only that, but everyone has stories within stories, stories with other people, stories connected to places, stories of experiences. The stories may lie forgotten in our consciousness until some little thing brings them to life again. For me last week, it was finding two small seashells in the pocket of my summer jacket. I'd stuck them there after Sally said, "We have so many shells; let's not collect any here." But I'm a sentimental fool at heart, so I put the two tiny shells in my pocket. That was six months ago. When I stuck my hand in and felt them, it brought back the whole story of the winter vacation on the beach in Florida—the walks, the seafood, Ronald feeding the seagulls, watching the dolphins, all of it. And I was grateful for those tiny trophies from the sea.

Think about your stories for which you are grateful. What can you do to bring them to life today?
—JAA

June 17

MY FATHER WAS A SOUTHERN Baptist minister; he was also an author and something of a poet like me. As pastor of a church in Memphis, Tennessee, in the 1930s, he wrote poems for the church newspaper and often for the order of worship bulletin.

After my mother's death, I found a group of these poems in a scrapbook I took from her house.

I had a sister who died when I was about two years old. She was disabled and unable to walk. Having a child with a disability myself, I felt even more connected to my father as I read this poem twenty years after he died. I was also struck again by the power of poetry to reach across the years.

In Memory of Ruth Evelyn Autry Who Died One Year Ago
Your chair is waiting up the Stairs,
Your books are waiting, too,
And in our hearts there is a spot
A-hungering for you.

Your rose is blooming by the wall;
It sheds its fragrance rare,
And in those rosebuds of the dawn
Your memory is there.

The flowers are blooming on your grave
And though you've gone to stay,
We're nearer you this very night
Than when you went away.

Be grateful today for whatever gives you a meaningful link to the past.

—JAA

June 18

I AM A FAN OF the Persian mystic poet Rumi. Perhaps my favorite little poem of his is this:

I, You, He, She, We.
In the garden of mystic lovers
these are not true distinctions.

What this means to me is that we can be part of that garden by suspending preconceptions and accepting everyone without judgment.

Has someone accepted you without judgment? Be grateful. And then go and show the same attitude toward someone else.

—JAA

June 19

"Happiness is like a butterfly which, when pursued, is always beyond our grasp, but, if you will sit down quietly, may alight upon you." (Nathaniel Hawthorne)

LIVING IN GRATITUDE INVITES the butterfly of happiness. Unfortunately, too many of us seem to think of happiness as if it were another consumer product that we can somehow possess. But it is a way of being that comes not from "out there" but from within ourselves, and as Mr. Hawthorne suggests, reveals itself to us when we let go of expectations and accept life as it is. Then we will discover that living in gratitude invites the butterfly of happiness.

Let that butterfly alight on you today.

—JAA

June 20

AFTER A VISIT TO the Grand Canyon a couple of years ago, I realized that our country has been richly blessed with visionary officials and leaders who could see the need for preserving and maintaining our natural treasures. I'm grateful that they were able to take on the task of enacting laws and providing resources for that good work all over the nation. And I'm grateful for the present-day public servants who keep those places ready for us to visit.

Show your gratitude and plan today to visit one of the national or state parks or monuments.

—JAA

June 21

I LIVED IN SWEDEN as an exchange student the summer after my high school graduation. My host family had a summer cottage on a lake where they customarily spent a few days celebrating the summer solstice.

Though I had visited northern Minnesota many times, I had never experienced a summer that far north, so the days of almost constant sunlight were new to me.

My Swedish "sister" shared an experience with me I will never forget. On June 21, sometime past midnight, we got in a small fishing boat, rowed out into the middle of the lake, and watched as the sun skimmed the horizon—slipping out of sight for a few minutes and then reemerging.

I had just watched both a sunset and a sunrise in a matter of minutes. It was quite breathtaking. Even these decades later, I still recall it with wonder.

Take time today to observe the wonders of a sunrise or sunset wherever you are, and be grateful for the life-giving sun.

—SJP

June 22

I LOVE TO TRAVEL, but once I'm at my destination, even the most interesting and exciting places on earth, it doesn't take long for me to be ready to head home. I can take only so much of unfamiliar beds, showers, and restaurant meals until the predictable everyday routines begin have more appeal than the next spectacular chateau, vineyard, waterfall, or mountain vista. Don't get me wrong. I am blessed to be able to travel, and I am grateful for it, but I am also grateful to have a welcoming home at the end of the travels.

Be grateful today for all of life's adventures, even the adventure of coming home.

—JAA

June 23

"A truly happy person is one who can enjoy the scenery while on a detour."
(author unknown)

I CONFESS THAT THIS quote hit me hard because it's difficult for me to relax and enjoy the scenery when some unexpected road repair backs up traffic and then sends me on a detour. The quote of course refers to the unexpected twists and turns that life takes, reminding me that there will always be the unexpected, the things I can do nothing about, and that living in gratitude is the best response. Gratitude allows me to enjoy all the scenery and circumstances of life.

Can you put aside your frustrations and be grateful for the unexpected?

—JAA

June 24

FROM A FRIEND:

"I am thankful for a mother who instilled the belief that, as much as possible, we are the custodians of our health. Now, as an 80-year-old who followed that admonition, I am grateful for being strong and healthy enough to be the primary care-giver for my 100-year-old husband of 54 years."

If you, too, are in good health, this would be a good time to pause and just be grateful for that.

—JAA

June 25

WHEN I GO TO reunions with people I've not seen in years, I suffer some cognitive dissonance because I inevitably have judgments and expectations based on who or how they were when I knew them versus how they seem to be now. People I had little to do with then turn out to be people with whom I want to spend more time now. Marcel Proust said, "Time, which changes people, does not alter the image we have retained of them." The challenge is to let go of those retained images and always be grateful and open to the people and circumstances as they presently are.

Can you open yourself to people as they are today, not as they were yesterday?

—JAA

June 26

SEVERAL YEARS AGO, IT became apparent to Sally and me and to parents of other young people with intellectual disabilities that, once they were no longer in school, these kids had precious little opportunity for social activities with others their age. We met in the office of a helpful therapist who had treated several of our young people. She'd been successful in setting up social gatherings and suggested that we let our young people participate in those and perhaps create others. Sally and I arranged for a room on Friday night at our church and established a "movie night." We got the word out to the parents and set up a schedule for chaperoning. The adults open the church and usually bring treats. The kids bring movies and choose among themselves which one to watch. The only rule we set was, "Nothing rated R or above."

So for several years, we've had a successful movie night with attendance as low as two or three and as high as ten or twelve. Friendships have formed so that the attendees stay in touch on Facebook and through texting and so on.

I am so grateful for the parents and young people who participate, for the hospitality of the church, and for the very fact that this arrangement works.

Be grateful today that we live in a society in which everyone has the opportunity to participate. And if you get a chance to help, do so.

—JAA

June 27

So many Gods, so many creeds,
So many paths that wind and wind,
While just the art of being kind
Is all the sad world needs.
(Ella Wheeler Wilcox)

SOMETIMES WE OVERTHINK HOW to improve the world, and the complexity of it all causes us to do nothing.

Show your gratitude today by simply being kind to someone who least expects it.

—SJP

June 28

"We must not, in trying to think about how we can make a big difference, ignore the small daily differences we can make, which over time add up to a big difference that we can not foresee." (Marian Wright Edelman)

MARIAN WRIGHT EDELMAN IS a remarkable woman whose life exemplifies the concept of making a difference. When she began advocating for children in the 1970s, she could not imagine that her work would occupy her for the next forty years or that her small efforts would grow into the nation's strongest voice for children and families, the Children's Defense Fund.

That, in fact, is the story of most successful movements or organizations. Each begins with one person committed to making a small difference and, over time, the accumulated effect can be life changing for that person and so many others.

What small difference can you make today? Be grateful for the opportunity and ability to do that small thing.

—SJP

June 29

OF ALL THE PLANTS I have, the most exotic and one of the most beautiful is the night-blooming cereus. As the name suggests, it blooms only at night, a large white blossom with a yellow center and a faintly lemony aroma. It is spectacular. Then, by daybreak, it begins to fade and closes. Fortunately, my plant is one of those with several blossoms, so I can always expect more blooms during the season. The trick is to monitor the large buds daily so I don't miss one night's bloom, and when we determine that the flower will appear that evening, it creates a bit of eager anticipation at our house. We've even invited the neighbors for a viewing. I am grateful for the rewarding variety of flowers, from the lowly crocus to the exotic cereus.

Do you love plants and flowers? Are you grateful for the beauty they add to life?

—JAA

June 30

IN THE PAST FEW years, the word "amazing" has become perhaps our society's most overused word. It's not that I'm against the word, but I'd prefer that it be applied to things that are truly amazing, such as the changing of seasons, a sunset, acts of kindness, the birth of a baby, the performance of a violin concerto, and the surge of gratitude that comes at those times when we are able to recognize the great mystery of our own amazing lives.

Be grateful for the things that truly amaze you.

—JAA

July 1

WE NATURALLY THINK OF justice as having to do with society and with the courts, and we are grateful for those institutions, but there is also personal justice—or fairness—in the way we go about our interests and in the way we treat others. It involves a balance that treats like things alike and different things differently, and it is often difficult to strike that balance. To live in gratitude, we also want others to have lives for which they are grateful.

Here's what others have said about justice and fairness:

"Legal justice is the art of the good and the fair." (Anonymous)

"Although I am a typical loner in daily life, my consciousness of belonging to the invisible community of those who strive for truth, beauty, and justice has preserved me from feeling isolated." (Albert Einstein)

"Fairness is what justice really is." (Potter Stewart)

"The aim of justice is to give everyone his due." (Cicero)

"Being good is easy, what is difficult is being just." (Victor Hugo)

Write down some of the ways, large and small, by which you can express gratitude by doing daily acts of justice and fairness.

—JAA

July 2

WIND CHIMES AND BELLS have been around for thousands of years. In ancient Rome, chimes were hung in gardens and porticoes to ward off evil spirits. Wind chimes and bells were popular in China and Japan and were thought to bring good luck.

Whether or not these ancient beliefs are true, I find that wind chimes and bells bring a special beauty and grace to their surroundings. Hanging among the tree limbs in our backyard, we have a small collection including a large bell that strikes a low gong, a metal chime with four long pipes that make a loud musical sound, and a barely audible tiny ring of cylinders suspended from a metal hummingbird.

There is something pleasant and magical about sitting quietly on our back patio and listening to the wind play these lovely instruments. The chimes make the wind visible to our ears, and the sound speaks to something deeper within us.

Are you grateful for something as simple as a wind chime that calls your attention to the wind and air you breathe every day?

—SJP

July 3

"WE COME TOGETHER TO be the best we can be, helping others to be the best they can be." This sentence is part of the mission statement of a company in Australia, and I believe it should be part of our own personal goals. I'm grateful that I got the chance, over several years, to work with this company and to help them shape their operating philosophy.

Today, consider whether you are trying to be the best you can be and what you can do to help others be the best they can be.

—JAA

July 4

THE DECLARATION OF INDEPENDENCE is a wonderful document, but I'd like it a little better if it said something other than "the pursuit of happiness." That makes it sound as if happiness is out there somewhere and we have to pursue it, chase it, run it down, and catch it. Happiness is not "out there"; it's "in here." Happiness comes from within us as we respond to whatever we perceive and receive as the conditions and situations that inspire our happiness. Abraham Lincoln said that people are as happy as they make up their minds to be. Put another way, if we are open to the possibilities of our own happiness, we'll be happy. It took me a while, but I'm grateful that I finally learned that truth.

Choosing gratitude is the same as choosing happiness. Think about that today.

—JAA

July 5

IN 1944, WENDELL WILLKIE said, "The Constitution does not provide for first and second class citizens." We are still struggling with our interpretations of the Constitution, but I am not only grateful for the Constitution; I am grateful for the struggle itself.

In this season of fireworks and parades and picnics and patriotic music, say a prayer of gratitude for the privilege of living in this country.

—JAA

July 6

TWO YEARS AGO, WE replaced some overgrown shrubs in our front yard with a hearty variety of roses popular in the Midwest, called Knockout roses.

There are nine bushes in all, five red and four hot pink, that bloom profusely from May until late October. Of course, to keep them in flower, we must deadhead the faded blossoms on a regular basis—at least once a week.

Strangely enough, I actually take pleasure in doing this job—standing amid the rosebushes, plucking the old blossoms and making way for the new. I think the small but regular attention required increases my overall enjoyment of these prolific beauties.

If you are a gardener, are you grateful for the opportunity to partner with nature in encouraging new growth? Are there other interests in your life that reward your attention with beauty?

—SJP

July 7

"To handle yourself, use your head; to handle others, use your heart." *(Eleanor Roosevelt)*

I HAVE WRITTEN SEVERAL books about leadership and management and have lectured in these subjects as well. When I read this quote by Mrs. Roosevelt, I thought, "If I had just quoted her, I could have saved myself a lot of words." Fundamentally, her advice applies to any kind of personal relationship—between spouses, parents and children, friends, or employers and employees.

Hers is the kind of wisdom for which I am consistently grateful.

When dealing with others, do you follow your heart?

—JAA

July 8

LIKE MANY PEOPLE, I keep a file of personal notes that have special meaning for me. Some of these are handwritten messages of congratulations for an achievement or milestone in my life. Others are notes of appreciation or kind words of encouragement that came at a particularly challenging time. Every now and then, I open and reread some of these messages from the past and reflect on what was happening at that time and the importance of those thoughtful friends and colleagues who wrote to me.

In this day of e-mail, instant messaging, texting, and tweeting, I wonder if the act of penning a personal note is a lost art. I tend to believe Marshall McLuhan had it right when he said, "The medium is the message." I treasure my handwritten notes because, by their very nature, they convey the writer's personal care and concern.

Today, take the time to write a personal note to someone for whom you care. The result is likely to be one of gratitude.

—SJP

July 9

WHEN I OPENED MY e-mail today, I saw the name of a man I'd not seen or thought about in a long time. It opened a flood of memories of times we worked together, of projects we accomplished together, and of my disappointment and anger when he suddenly left our company to take a job in another town.

He's in town today and wants to get together for coffee. The decision to meet him made me focus on the gratitude I feel for the good times we had and let go of the residual disappointment. I confess that it took some effort, but it liberated me from any negative feelings. I'm looking forward to our get-together and am grateful he contacted me.

What grudge or anger may you be holding on to that might be dissolved by an attitude of gratitude?

—JAA

July 10

I OFTEN MEET PEOPLE who say, "I'm working on a book." I always have to resist asking, "Yes, but are you writing one?"

It is easy to delude ourselves by substituting intention for action. I am grateful that I finally have matured beyond being disappointed for what I have not done and am happy with what I am doing now.

Can you let go of your grand intentions and be grateful for what you do now?

—JAA

July 11

"Happiness is when what you think, what you say, and what you do are in harmony." (Mahatma Gandhi)

I'VE KNOWN PEOPLE WHO were adept at saying one thing and doing another. Not only that—they were also proud of it and used it as a strategy in dealing with people. But it doesn't work over the long term. Watching them, I learned that if my actions and my values were not in alignment, then I would make other people unhappy and end up unhappy myself. I don't believe I could live in gratitude and not have my values and actions aligned.

This would be a good day for an alignment check. Be grateful if you say what you're going to do then do what you said you'd do.

—JAA

July 12

FOR MOST OF MY life, I tried to deal with what I called "the great existential conflict" between what I wanted to do and what I thought I ought to want to do. I finally came to realize that persisting in that conflict simply postponed the living of life and deprived me of gratitude for the life I was already living. After that, I began to find that what I wanted to do was also what I ought to do. Imagine that.

Be grateful if you've managed to let go of what you thought you wanted and have come to appreciate what you have.

—JAA

July 13

MY NIECE SARAH IS in thirty-eight and expecting her first child. She has wanted a family for a long time, so we are all very excited for her.

Later today, I am going to box up a floral-print maternity top and mail it to her. I wore this smock when I was pregnant with my son thirty years ago. It was a special gift from my mother—Sarah's grandmother—who wore it when she was pregnant with me back in the early 1950s. I guess that makes this garment more than sixty years old. I think, in fact, that it is old enough to be back in style—at least I hope Sarah thinks so.

But, whether she wears it or not, I know she will appreciate the love and feminine power that inhabits this special piece of clothing and will treasure it as I have.

I don't know why I have kept this maternity top hanging in my closet for all these years. I guess I couldn't imagine discarding it or giving it away. Now, this pretty smock has a new mother to adorn and a family story to go with it.

Family heirlooms come in many forms. Are you grateful for small things that may carry big memories?

—SJP

July 14

"In the deepest night of trouble and sorrow God gives us so much to be thankful for that we need never cease our singing." (Samuel Taylor Coleridge)

IT IS INEVITABLE THAT, at some time in our lives, we will have deep nights of trouble and sorrow, and we respond in various ways. My son Jimmy has been a model for me in the past few years. He struggled for years with addiction. Indeed, he had many of those "deepest nights of trouble and sorrow," yet in the midst of his dark times he had other times of introspection and creativity in which he was able to write poetry and express the smallest light of gratitude and hope. One of his poems appears in this book as the April 5 entry.

Even in your dark times, try to find gratitude for the hope that's always there.

—JAA

July 15

I ONCE HEARD A poet friend say that he was tired of all the violent imagery. For instance, he pointed out, the scientists talk about the "big bang" theory. He suggested that instead of thinking of the universe beginning as a bomb, why not think of it as a flower bulb or seed? Then, rather than a big bang theory, we'd have the big bloom theory, with the universe expanding because it is still coming into bloom.

That image more likely inspires gratitude for the mystery of creation. Don't you agree?

—JAA

July 16

I'VE PERSONALLY WITNESSED SEVERAL situations when police officers have made an extra effort to help someone. These did not involve criminal activity, but everyday things like a car having mechanical problems and, in one case, an elderly person who obviously was confused and lost. When my son Ronald had a minor car wreck last year, he became very agitated. The investigating police officer obviously sensed Ronald's autism and calmly told him that, since no one was hurt, it was not a big problem. Then the officer guided Ronald through all the paperwork and so on. I arrived in the middle of this and soon determined that my help was not needed. The officer was sensitive not only to Ronald's disability but also to the need to treat him like an adult. Once again, I found myself grateful for those who "protect and serve." They have a difficult and often dangerous job, and I try to make it a habit, when I have the chance, to say "thank you for your service" to a police officer.

Are you grateful for those who protect and serve? Why don't you thank one of them today?

—JAA

July 17

QIGONG IS AN ANCIENT Chinese practice that combines breathing, movement, and awareness. My Qigong teacher begins each class with a visualization that her teacher taught her.

We put a smile on our faces, and then we imagine moving the smile inside our heads and inside our whole bodies.

Try it. You don't need to practice Qigong to adopt this exercise. If you are smiling inside, you can't help but feel gratitude for the universe.

—SJP

July 18

"We must use time wisely and forever realize that the time is always ripe to do the right thing." (Nelson Mandela)

NELSON MANDELA SPENT TWENTY-SEVEN years in prison in South Africa, never giving up his struggle to end apartheid. In 1990, he was released from prison and worked to bring full citizenship to black South Africans and majority rule to his country. In 1994 at the age of seventy-seven, he became the first black president of South Africa.

Nelson Mandela was born on July 18, 1918. In 2009, his birthday was declared Mandela Day to celebrate his legacy and promote global peace.

Today, give thanks for leaders who recognize that "the time is always ripe" and who move humanity toward greater justice and equality.

—SJP

July 19

"Use what talents you possess; the woods would be very silent if no birds sang there except those that sang best." (Henry van Dyke)

I HAVE A FRIEND who, as we used to say, "can't carry a tune in a bucket," yet he sings with great gusto. It used to irritate me because I convinced myself that it hurt my ears and that I shouldn't have to tolerate it. I think now about what an intolerant jerk I was. The point of singing is to make a joyful noise and enjoy it, and if the result sounds good to the singer, then it is good enough for me. I'm now grateful for anyone these days who is willing to raise a voice in song.

Be grateful if you like to sing, and let your voice ring out today.

—JAA

July 20

MANY YEARS AGO, I brought some little garlic plants from my late mother's garden in Mississippi. They have thrived, proving my mother's comment when I was carefully packing them for the driving trip to Iowa. "Don't worry," she said. "You can't kill them." Indeed. Now I have more garlic plants that I can keep up with. The only reason I keep them at all is that they remind me of my mother's garden. Why else would I? It's a little irrational. After all, I'm allergic to garlic.

Have you irrationally saved things just because you are grateful for the memories they inspire?

—JAA

July 21

HERE'S A LESSON IN gratitude from friend and poet Phil Hey:

Cleaning the chimney
Approaching 71, I have to clean the creosote out of my chimney;
I have the brushes, the gloves, the ladder, and even a rope
tied firmly to a leg of the antenna to help me up and down the roof.
What I may not have any more is the balance or the nerve to test it.
Still my great-grandmother at 91 picked her own cherries
from a tree she planted beside her house, setting up
her own ladder fearlessly. (And never fell, that I heard of.)
I remember her silver-gray hair and her toothy grin in the sun
as she stood in front of her house, and now I have the same color of hair
and as strong a motive to go up the ladder. Well, if she could do it,
then I can. And now I have to work on the grin.

Do you have an older loved one who has set an example for which you are grateful?

—JAA

July 22

"Forgiveness is the fragrance that the violet sheds on the heel that has crushed it." (Mark Twain)

IT TOOK ME A while to learn that I must recognize that there are two sides to forgiveness if I am to live in gratitude. First, I must be grateful for the strength I can muster to forgive someone. Then comes the hard part: I must be grateful for that person's willingness to let me forgive.

Think about it. Can you be grateful for the willingness to be forgiven?

—JAA

July 23

I HAD A FRIEND a few years ago who used to say, "Friends are the new family." My friend's point was that we have become a mobile society in which families often become separated by many miles. People find themselves in need of the intimacy and support families usually provide, so they turn to friends. Apparently, however, the idea of friends as family is not new. Eustache Deschamps, writing in the fifteenth century, said, "Friends are relatives you make for yourself." Indeed, I have friends who are as close as family and as supportive as family. I am grateful for them.

Do you have friends who are like family and who will stick with you through anything? Let them know how grateful you are for them.

—JAA

July 24

DO YOU NEED A quick, ten-second gratitude fix? Here's a little exercise I do whenever I get overly stressed or preoccupied during a day. I've also used this in workshops on organizational leadership. Try it.

Close your eyes. Take a deep breath and hold it. Think of something that will always make you smile, a child perhaps, or a pet, or the memory of a vacation—anything that makes you smile. Then think about it, smile, open your eyes, and exhale. I guarantee you'll immediately feel better, more relaxed or less stressed.

Try this little exercise three times today. When you discover how well it works, teach it to someone else. They'll be grateful you did.

—JAA

July 25

HELEN KELLER, WHO WAS without sight or hearing, once said, "Of all the senses, sight must be the most delightful."

Have you ever been asked to consider which sense you'd give up if you had such a choice? It's a question that tries to make us decide which of our senses is most vital to us. I can't do it. I am grateful for all my senses and can't imagine being without one of them, yet I know many people who've lost one or more and who not only survive but seem to thrive. I have undying gratitude for them and the example they set for all of us.

Be grateful today for whatever senses you have and for the example of those who live admirable lives while deprived of one or more.

—JA

July 26

I LISTENED TO A compact disc the other day that made me grateful. It was of a group of friends, including me, who started getting together to play swing and traditional jazz. We called ourselves "The Over the Hill Jazz Band." It was just for fun, but we got good enough that we began to play, at no charge, for groups and parties. This went on for several years and became a great joy in all our lives. I wouldn't take anything for that experience. The group has become scattered, but a couple of its members still perform seriously (they were always the best musicians of the bunch). My part now consists only of listening to the CD and remembering those great times.

Can you be grateful just for the fun you've had?

—JAA

July 27

I RECENTLY WENT TO the wedding of a friend's daughter. It was a joyful event, as most weddings are, but the joy of this one extended well into the reception. There were all ages of people, from toddlers to great-grandfolks. After the toasts and testimonials, the dancing began. I've seen some people dancing in my day, but these were the happiest, most uninhibited folks I've ever seen. I think a lot of it had to do with the mix of ages. It seemed to me that the older people, taking a cue from the younger set, were letting their inner children loose and giving them permission to play with the other kids, and both groups appreciated the other. I was grateful to be in that happy crowd.

Can you give your inner child permission to have fun today? If so, be grateful for that gift.

—JAA

July 28

I LIKE TO BARBECUE. I don't mean just throwing some meat on the grill and burning it a while; I mean a pork shoulder cooked over low heat and smoke for several hours, then pulled from the bone, chopped, and served with a good secret-recipe sauce. What makes this a particularly joyful activity in our family is the good-natured competition between me and one of my brothers-in-law as to who cooks the best barbecue. As someone raised in the South, I have a natural advantage over my Iowa-bred brother-in-law, but I try not to rub it in. As you can guess, we laugh a lot. I love this warm-weather ritual and the opportunity to express my gratitude (and love) with barbecue.

Be grateful for the rituals with your family and friends, and if you don't have any rituals, this would be a good day to cook one up.

—JAA

July 29

"It is only with the heart that one can see clearly. What's essential is invisible to the eye." (from The Little Prince, *by Antoine de St. Exupery)*

I AGREE WITH THE author, but the question naturally arises, "How can we see with the heart?" I think the answer depends partly on who is doing the seeing and what they are looking for. Lovers? Of course they see one another with the heart because they are engaged intensely with matters of the heart. What about the rest of us? How do we see with the heart? I believe the phrase means that when we can see the world and the people in it with a spirit of openness, acceptance, and compassion, we will be seeing with the heart. And that's something to work toward and be grateful for.

Are you able to look at the world with your heart as well as your eyes?

—JAA

July 30

ON TRAVELS IN THE past few years, I've been astounded by the night sky. Once on Lord Howe Island, Australia, where there are no streetlights, the night sky seemed so close that I felt surrounded by it. On a guest ranch in northern Colorado, I had the same experience. These experiences made me realize how much of the sky I never see. Of course I appreciate my city's lights, but for a dose of night sky gratitude, I have to drive out in the country occasionally.

For a gratitude experience, try to get away from the streetlights this evening and just look up.

—JAA

July 31

"Care what other people think and you will always be their prisoner."
(Lao Tzu)

IT'S DIFFICULT NOT TO care what other people think. We are almost conditioned in our society to be overly sensitive to what other people think, what other people like, what other people wear, what car they drive, where they vacation, and on and on. We are bombarded with commercial messages that seduce us into comparing ourselves to other people and thus caring about what they think of us or would think of us if they knew us. If we give in to this way of thinking, we become as the wise Lao Tzu said, the prisoner of other people and their opinions. I confess that it took me a long time to liberate myself from this flaw in my thinking, but I have, and I'm grateful that I have.

Do you find yourself drawn into the trap of caring what other people think? Be grateful that it is in your power to liberate yourself from becoming their prisoner.

—JAA

August 1

BEGIN THIS MONTH WITH gratitude for compassion and the acts that flow from it. There is personal compassion and there is institutional compassion, and most of us can find opportunities in our churches or community organizations to participate in both.

Read what others have said about compassion:

"Compassion is not weakness, and concern for the unfortunate is not socialism." (Hubert Humphrey)

"A certain Samaritan . . . had compassion on him." (Luke 10:33)

"Compassion, which can be aroused quickly, is often difficult to maintain; it is a great virtue precisely because it is not an easy one." (Rick Autry)

"He [man] is immortal, not because he alone among creatures has an inexhaustible voice, but because he has a soul, a spirit capable of compassion and sacrifice and endurance." (William Faulkner)

Now write about acts of compassion you have witnessed or heard or read about.

—JAA

August 2

MY SON RONALD IS a true romantic. He loves watching old movies with boy-meets-girl plot lines and happily-ever-after endings. His favorite singers are those famous for old-fashioned love songs, and he sprinkles his language with phrases like "your eyes sparkle like diamonds" and "your lips are like rubies."

For several years he has been in serious and persistent search of a girlfriend, asking friends for help, joining online dating services, and attending meet-ups. None of these led anywhere. But recently, he attended a friend's birthday party where he reconnected with an old acquaintance. They started dating and immediately hit it off. They both seem love-struck, and time will tell if it is the real thing.

For now, though, he is totally in love, and he shares the news widely. And so do his father and I. It seems that joy is one of those emotions that is hard to contain. We are amused by Ronald's obsession with "notifying" all his friends and relatives of his new relationship, as well as the bank clerk, the supermarket cashier, and the neighbor he meets while walking his dog. But we too find ourselves telling most anyone who offhandedly asks about Ronald the details of his new romance. It makes us happy to see him so full of love and hope.

Are there people you know who are experiencing falling in love? Be grateful for the joy of new love and the universal desire to share that joy with others.

—SJP

August 3

"The essential sadness is to go through life without loving. But it would be almost equally sad to leave this world without ever telling those you loved that you love them." (Anonymous)

WHATEVER THERE IS TO do today, there is nothing more important than expressing your love to someone. The second most important thing is telling someone that you are grateful for his or her presence in the world.

Is there someone you should call and say, "I'm grateful for you today"? If so, go and do that now.

—JAA

August 4

"There are no shortcuts to anyplace worth going." (Helen Keller)

THIS IS A QUOTE from a person who was without sight or hearing as a result of a childhood illness. Helen Keller not only found no shortcuts but also had to go the long way and the hard way throughout her remarkable life. Yet she was a person of gratitude and thus set an example for the rest of us on how to succeed without shortcuts in whatever we set ourselves to do. Whenever I get frustrated by details or by how long a project is taking, I try to think of her and be grateful for her memory and her lesson that life does not always give us the easy way.

If you feel frustrated today by how difficult something is, think of Helen Keller. Be grateful for what you can do and let go of what you can't do.

—JAA

August 5

MY COLLEAGUE, LAURA RIORDAN BERARDI, shared this story with me:

> This is a hard story for me to tell. This is not me at my best, but it's one of the best lessons, reminders . . . and blessings . . . I have experienced.
>
> I was probably in my mid-twenties at the time, and I was out with friends for drinks and conversation and general silliness. Nick had half a watermelon with him. I don't remember why, just that he was hauling it around the bar with him, offering it to people, but with no takers. Later that night, as we were leaving the bar with a group of friends, Nick carried the watermelon out with him.
>
> We were walking to another bar when a woman approached us, asking for money. We all declined her request, using the cover of the group to keep talking, keep moving. Nick, though, offered her the watermelon. She stopped and looked at him, obviously disappointed in the offer. But ultimately she took it, and we moved on.
>
> Later on the way to our cars we passed the woman again, but this time she was sitting in a doorway, and she was devouring the watermelon with a plastic spoon. My stomach turned at the sight. It was at that moment I saw her not as someone who was begging on the streets, but as someone who was hungry. And, except for some leftover melon, we had all passed her by. I turned back, digging a few dollars out of my pocket.
>
> I remembered something I had once read: "When someone less fortunate needs help, it is not up to us to pass judgment on them, on their circumstances, on what we *think* they might use the money for. If we are able to help, if we have been so blessed in this life that we are able to help others, then that is what we do."

Are you grateful for the many opportunities you have had in life, especially for opportunities to help others?

—SJP

August 6

I WAS DELIGHTED TO get an e-mail the other day from a friend, Pam, who seldom writes. The occasion that prompted the message was a "corgi sighting."

She was forwarding a photo from her daughter in Washington D.C. who had snapped a picture of a tricolor corgi she had seen on a walk. My friend's own tricolor corgi died last year after a long and faithful life. Her daughter sent the cell phone photo as a way of remembering their dog. Pam forwarded it to me because my grand-dog is a tricolor. Of course, I passed it along to the dog owner, Ronald.

My husband and I have dubbed such happenings "corgi sightings." If we spot a corgi, we snap a photo with our cell phone or at a minimum make a mental note and report the sighting to Ronald. It may seem silly to others, but for some dog lovers, this shared moment brightens the day.

Are you grateful for others who share your love for one of God's creations?

—SJP

August 7

RECENTLY, I HAD COFFEE with a man who worked in my group many years ago. He'd gone on to another career and had returned to town for a visit. I'd not seen him in at least a decade. He called and we got together. Part of the conversation was about how I had given him assignments that taught him things he used later in his career. He shook my hand and thanked me warmly. I think of that as bread upon the waters.

Is there someone you knew years ago whom you should thank today—or at least think about with gratitude?

—JAA

August 8

READ THESE WORDS OF comfort from Christian mystic Julian of Norwich:

> And all shall be well . . .
> And all shall be well . . .
> And all manner of things shall be well . . .

Can you allow yourself to believe these words today?

—JAA

August 9

MY FRIEND MARTI HAS been volunteering at a hospice facility near her home for some time. She washes the soiled sheets of the patients who are living out their final weeks and days in palliative care.

When she first signed on to help at the center, she expected something different, though she's not sure just what. "I wanted to be involved in the spiritual aspect of people who are at the end of their lives," Marti told me. Yet she was willing to work where she was needed. What she discovered was that the very job of cleaning up the unpleasant mess that comes with the human body in its final stages had a spiritual meaning for her. She goes about her volunteer work with purpose and with a real feeling of compassion and love.

Every act of caring has a spiritual dimension. Can you find a sense of compassion and gratitude in the most mundane of tasks?

—SJP

August 10

"It takes a strong person to say sorry, and an even stronger person to forgive." (author unknown)

MY SON RONALD HAS his quirks, and one of them is his need for a specific response when he says he's sorry about something. It's not sufficient for me to say, "That's okay" or "I forgive you." I must say, in these exact words, "I accept your apology." If I don't, he tells me, "Say 'I accept your apology.'" His transgressions are always minor, and I never think of them as requiring forgiveness; nonetheless, he needs to feel that I have forgiven him. I'm grateful for this little ritual with Ronald because it reminds me that we all need forgiveness from time to time.

Do you need to forgive someone today? Do you need someone's forgiveness today?

—JAA

August 11

WHEN WE RETIRE, WE can either let ourselves be slaves to the past or be liberated. We are liberated when we see ourselves as an accumulation of all the experiences, good and bad, we've ever had; all the people we've ever known; and all the things we've ever done—and when we see that none of it is lost. We are liberated in knowing that all of it has been part of the great adventure that nurtured us into who we are today.

Today, I am grateful for this person: _____
this experience: _____
and this accomplishment: _____.

—JAA

August 12

A **FORMER COLLEAGUE OF** mine, Laurie, took several weeks off work last year to walk the Camino de Santiago in Spain. It is a pilgrimage that ends at the Cathedral of Santiago de Compostela, the burial site of the remains of St. James, and, depending on where one starts, it can take weeks or months to travel.

More than 100,000 people from all over the world make this pilgrimage every year. Like many of them, Laurie felt changed by the experience.

Over coffee, she described the wisdom she learned from one Camino pilgrim she met as she walked:

> The Camino (The Way) is an analogy of our journey in life. What are the real meanings behind "in the way," "on the way," and "by the way"? If we step back from the flip notions of these phrases, we may consider them as rules to live by.
>
> In the way: Be present. Aware. Listen. And in each case to do this for self and others you meet.
>
> On the way: You have goals. You know that each step is getting you further along. Movement. Growth. Progress.
>
> By the way: The path you have chosen . . . the Way . . . living your life with purpose.

I felt privileged that Laurie would share her hard-earned wisdom with me, and in some small way I felt connected to her journey.

Who are your fellow pilgrims on life's journey? Are you grateful for their companionship?

—SJP

August 13

THE GREAT WILLIAM SLOANE COFFIN once said that Socrates was mistaken. "It's not the unexamined life that is not worth living," Coffin said. "It's the uncommitted life."

Let's be grateful today for the people who have made commitments in their lives. Have you?

—JAA

August 14

ON THE GREAT PLAINS where I live, summer is a time of the many shades of green. Out in farmland, the fields lie in geometric shapes across the landscape, and I take great pleasure in how, next to a field of soybeans, the tall corn rises at a right angle. Recently I was moved to write this poem that expresses my gratitude for this beautiful country.

Summer
It is early.
I am driving northeast.
The sun skims the soybeans,
the corn rises from the ground
like a green wall at the end of the bean field
at an angle that's right in every way,
a comfort, an affirmation
of the dependability of things
good and growing.

Are you grateful today for all the bounty and beauty of the earth and for the dependability of things?

—JAA

August 15

I RECEIVED A LONG, newsy, and very welcome letter from an old colleague today. Yes, it was handwritten in ink, on paper, and somehow that made it an even more personal connection. I was grateful not only for the contents of the letter but also for the physical presence of the letter itself. Now it's my turn to take the time to sit down and answer it.

Why don't you take time to write an old-fashioned handwritten letter today that expresses your gratitude for a friend or loved one?

—JAA

August 16

MY FRIEND DAVID JORDAN and I were discussing people's responses to the diagnosis of a fatal disease, and he told me a story he'd heard on the radio. It was about a farmer who, after hearing such a diagnosis and learning he had but a few weeks to live, returned to the farm and immediately changed into his field clothes. When asked what he was doing, he replied, "I'm going to hitch the horses and then do some plowing. Those horses have been idle, and they just need to pull." When David said these words, he became emotional, as did I. The message, of course, was not that the horses needed to pull but that the farmer needed to plow. David and I both came from people like that farmer; we understood his quiet desire to see to the needs of the horses rather than admit his own needs. And I think the plowing itself was an act of gratitude, even in the face of death, for the good work that had defined his life and given it meaning.

Are you grateful today for the work that has given your life meaning?

—JAA

August 17

"Rules for Happiness: something to do, someone to love, something to hope for." (Immanuel Kant)

IN MY FIRST BOOK about business, I offered this advice for success: "Find your people, find your place, do your work." That was very much like Kant's rules for happiness, and I suggest that these definitions of success and happiness also define a life of gratitude.

If you have found your place and your people, and if you are doing something that feeds your soul, then by all means be grateful.

—JAA

August 18

I'M JUST BACK FROM a long driving trip, and I find myself grateful for all the traveler support in this country: good highways, rest stops, and emergency services, all provided by government. Most of us don't give this a spare thought. Accompanying the good infrastructure, of course, is a myriad of private sector services: motels, restaurants, service stations, towing and repair services, not to mention recreational facilities and attractions. Oh, I know I could find something to criticize and complain about, but none of it outweighs what I can find to praise.

Are there some things you take for granted but that you also should be grateful for?

—JAA

August 19

CONVERSATIONS WITH OUR SON Ronald can be exceedingly narrow and repetitive. He has an intense interest in certain topics and never tires of talking about them. (Maybe we are all a little autistic in this way, but believe me, he goes to an extreme.)

I recently listened to my stepson Rick engage his half-brother, Ronald, in a somewhat lengthy conversation about a favorite subject, the Three Stooges. Rick said, "I like the one about Moe, when he is trying to get Curly and Larry to . . . ," and then he launched into a detailed description of the silly plot of one of the Stooges' many films. Ronald followed every word as Rick recounted the story, laughing now and then and occasionally adding a piece to the tale. Ronald was totally mesmerized for thirty or forty minutes.

Rick may not share Ronald's obsessive interest in the Three Stooges, but his brotherly love and generous spirit moves him to make the effort to engage Ronald on his own ground.

It is a pleasure to witness.

Today, pay attention to the subjects that interest others. Be willing to engage on their terms and give yourself fully to the conversation. You will be grateful you did.

—SJP

August 20

FROM A FRIEND:

"I'm grateful for the women who divide the altar flowers each Sunday and deliver them to shut-ins with a note that reads, 'These flowers are sent to you from the altar of St. Peter's Church to let you know you are remembered there. May they bring something of the peace of God's House and Presence.'"

Name the small acts of kindness for which you are grateful.

—JAA

August 21

MY FRIEND BILL CONNET has many talents. The one I appreciate most is how, as a volunteer, he uses his voice and his guitar to bring pleasure and comfort to elderly people in care facilities. He told me a wonderful story about an experience that not only moved him emotionally but also taught him a lesson about the power of music. At one appearance, the staff people brought in a lady in a wheelchair. Bill, who has some medical training, said, "I recognized the signs of dementia, but I wanted to somehow reach her." After performing a while, Bill decided to play music his audience might easily recognize and relate to. So he played "Amazing Grace." To everyone's amazement, the woman in the wheelchair began to sing. It's an experience for which Bill expresses deep gratitude. Amazing grace indeed.

Consider today the many people in all kinds of care facilities, and say a prayer of gratitude for the volunteers who work to bring some joy into their lives.

—JAA

August 22

WHEN I ASKED A COLLEAGUE what she'd studied in college, she said, "ecology." I replied, "Sounds like a big subject." She smiled and said, "I did my thesis on the study of one cubic yard of soil, and I learned much of what there is to know about ecology." It struck me that hers was a scientific approach to the famous William Blake poem about seeing eternity in a grain of sand. I confess that I sometimes become so preoccupied with my gratitude for life's important big things, such as friends and family, work and recreation, that I forget to focus on the small everyday things in nature that make life so rich.

Take a leisurely walk in your garden or a park today, and see what nature reveals to you.

—JAA

August 23

AS A YOUNG WRITER, I succumbed to the curse of falling in love with what I'd written and wasn't too receptive to criticism because I was ready to move on to the next thing. It took a while to learn that not everything I wrote was good. In fact, most of my early writing was bad, but I was anxious to do more of it. It seems to me that I was caught in what we now call "multi-tasking," trying to do too much at the same time rather than taking time to do one thing well. Alfred Nobel put it this way: "If I have a thousand ideas and only one turns out to be good, I'm satisfied."

Trying to live in gratitude has led me to focus more on the "how" of doing something rather than the result.

Do you sometimes get caught up in trying to do too many things at one time? Today, take time to slow down and focus on doing one good thing for which you can be grateful.

—JAA

August 24

ONE OF MY GREAT flaws has been that I've always hated to make mistakes, and when I do so I tend to beat up on myself. I go through a dozen iterations of "why didn't I do it this or that way." I sometimes just have to take deep breaths and try to be grateful that none of my mistakes proves serious and that I always seem to get another chance. There's a George Bernard Shaw quote I should put on my office wall: "A life spent making mistakes is not only more honorable, but more useful than a life spent doing nothing."

Take Mr. Shaw's advice today. Try something you've wanted to try, and be grateful that even if you make a mistake, you're living an honorable life.

—JAA

August 25

THIS MORNING I MET with two young women, Melissa and Heidi, to learn about a new program they are attempting to launch. Melissa told me the story of her son, Jack, who suffered a stroke at age nine. He had been an enthusiastic athlete and refused to give up sports despite his new physical challenges.

Special Olympics was not the answer, since its mission and focus is limited to children and adults with intellectual disabilities.

So Melissa decided to start a program for kids who need adaptive equipment and programming to participate in sports. Jack named the program "Courage League Sports." Melissa's friend Heidi is a pediatrician who serves on the board of their newly incorporated nonprofit.

They shared with me a well-formulated plan for establishing Courage League Sports and raising money to get it started. They are already a third of the way to their goal of $300,000 and I am confident that they will reach or exceed it.

Let's be grateful today for the people who, when adversity closes a door in their face, find a way to open a window for us all.

—SJP

August 26

TODAY I CHOSE SOME nice steaks to put on the grill this evening. Seeing all the meat at the supermarket flashed my memory back to my childhood during World War II when I accompanied my mother to the store and watched her carefully pull the rationing book from her purse. As I recall, meat and sugar were both rationed. Bananas were a luxury, and we kids always made a rush to the store when the precious candy bars arrived. We should not forget those days and should strive to be grateful for the abundance with which we are now blessed.

Have you experienced times of scarcity? Be grateful for these times of abundance.

—JAA

August 27

FOR SEVERAL YEARS, OUR family vacationed annually at a guest ranch in Colorado. The days were spent horseback riding, hiking, and fishing, with plenty of mountain air, sunshine, and good food.

The evenings provided special experiences as well. The ranch was located in the Elk River valley at an elevation of 7,200 feet—well above anything in our home state of Iowa. We were both figuratively and literally closer to the stars.

On several crystal-clear nights, we stayed up late to stargaze. We were never disappointed in the night sky performance. We could easily see the Milky Way and even identify, with the help of one of the better-informed ranch guests, the teapot-shaped constellation that pours the billions of Milky Way stars into the galaxy.

On one memorable night, we witnessed dozens of shooting stars flame across the blue-black sky, a performance that made me realize what a speck I am in the universe and at the same time made me feel special and enormously grateful.

Find the time to observe the night sky and contemplate the vastness of the universe. Be grateful for your special place in it.

—SJP

August 28

THERE ARE FRIENDS WITH whom I seem to have an almost mystical connection. For instance, I rarely see or even talk with my friend Jim Ferguson, but when we do make a connection by phone, the conversation continues as if we'd talked just yesterday. The time out of contact creates no gap in the connection, and we still feel close to one another. In 1981 when my father died, I called Jim. He said nothing but began to cry. We quickly said goodbye.

To explain what happened next, I need to say that, at the time, Jim was the well-known band director of the University of Alabama band. A few days after our conversation, I received a package in the mail, an audiotape, with no explanation. I put it in the player and could tell from the sound quality that it had been recorded outdoors. It was the Alabama band playing "Amazing Grace." Jim explained later that the band was practicing for its football halftime show and that he passed out the music for "Amazing Grace" and said, "People, I know we don't have time for anything extra, but this is very important to me. Let's try to do this on the first try."

Jim is a friend for whom I've been grateful since college days, and you can imagine how grateful I am for that recorded tribute to my father, which I've now put on a CD for safe keeping. (By the way, Jim used "Amazing Grace" for the finale of the band's half-time show at the Cotton Bowl that year, bringing 80,000 people to their feet.)

Be grateful for friends who are there through thick and thin, even if you don't see them often.

—JAA

August 29

RONALD, FROM THE TIME he could talk, always wanted to be an airline pilot. He was fascinated with airliners and was so good at identifying them that his schoolmates in elementary school would ask, "Ronald, what kind of airplane is that?" when one flew over the playground.

We bought him a flight simulator for his computer; he mastered that, but it wasn't enough. One day I said to my wife, "Who am I to rain on his parade? I'm going to find a flight instructor who will work with him."

Well, Ronald will not be an airline pilot. His autism makes that impossible, but he does have 200 flying hours and over 300 landings, always with his flight instructor, a patient and supportive man named Tom Ballard, who told us that Ronald is a very competent pilot. Tom taught Ronald to make instrument approaches and to do the radio exchanges with the approach control and tower.

I was listening on the radio one day, and when the approach control operator "handed off" Ronald to the control tower, the controller said, "Cleared to contact the tower on one eighteen point three. Have a good day, Ron." Imagine that.

A year or so ago, Tom Ballard decided to retire. After the last flight with Ronald, Tom said to me, "I think Ronald has taught me more than I taught him." It was a moving moment that I'll never forget.

Surely there is in your life a teacher, a pastor, a friend, or a boss for whom you feel that same gratitude that I feel for Tom Ballard.

—JAA

CHOOSING GRATITUDE

August 30

IT IS EASY TO deride groups of people with language that denigrates or reduces them to objects of scorn. It is far more difficult to do so once we personally know someone who is part of that group. Using words like "nigger," "queer," or "kike" has become taboo, largely because our society is more integrated than ever before. But it has also required leaders who speak out about the power of language and the need for mutual respect.

One such campaign is going on now to end the use of the word "retard" or "retarded" as a slur or term of ridicule. The most eloquent case for ending such offensive language is made by John Franklin Stephens, a man with Down syndrome who serves as a global messenger for the Special Olympics.

"So, what's wrong with 'retard'?" he asked. "I can only tell you what it means to me and people like me when we hear it. It means that the rest of you are excluding us from your group. We are something that is not like you and something that none of you would ever want to be. We are something outside the 'in' group. We are someone that is not your kind."

Cruel words, indeed!

Are you thoughtful about the words you choose? Are you grateful for the power of words to embrace, not exclude, others?

—SJP

August 31

"I AM SORRY."

Those are three of the most powerful words ever spoken. Yet it seems that they are also three of the most difficult words to speak. Why? The answer probably boils down to one word, "ego." In my leadership consulting work, I've often been asked, "What's the greatest barrier to good leadership?" I respond, "What's the greatest barrier to good friendships, good parenting, good relationships of any kind? Ego."

Ego somehow makes us believe that to admit a mistake or to say "I'm sorry" diminishes us, takes away part of what we perceive to be our power. Nonsense. The willingness to admit mistakes demonstrates the power of character and decency. It demonstrates "power with" not "power over." I know it works not only in leadership but in all relationships.

If you have so overcome your ego that you are able to say "I'm sorry" and mean it, then be grateful for this significant sign of your spiritual maturity.

—JAA

September 1

ARE WE HONEST? THE great majority of us would answer, "Yes." Do we always tell the truth? I suspect that the "yes" answers would quickly fall into the minority. Why is that? The answer starts by acknowledging that truth telling is only part of honesty. We must also acknowledge that unabashed, uninhibited, insensitive, tactless, and pointless truth telling loses its claim as a virtue when it hurts others, thus doing more harm than good. Most of us measure our words and their potential impact on others, and we regularly withhold the "truth" when we judge that it will serve no purpose other than diminishing someone. This is always a judgment call, but we can't equate radical and hurtful truth telling with the nobler aspects of honest living.

Honesty is fundamentally about our relationships with others and with the world, and just as we have to work to live in gratitude, we have to work at honest living.

Read now what others have written about honesty:

"To believe in something, and not to live it, is dishonest." (Mahatma Gandhi)

"If you do not tell the truth about yourself you cannot tell it about other people." (Virginia Woolf)

"Treat those who are good with goodness, and also treat those who are not good with goodness. Thus goodness is attained. Be honest to those who are honest, and be also honest to those who are not honest. Thus honesty is attained." (Lao Tzu)

"Honesty is the first chapter of the book wisdom." (Thomas Jefferson)

Write down your own thoughts and ideas about living a life of honesty and gratitude, and then share them with someone you love.

—JAA

September 2

I ONCE HEARD A man who'd been a chaplain at a home for the elderly describe the first time he entered the facility. Many of the residents had assembled in the large lounge. Some were in wheelchairs, others had walkers, and some stood as he entered. He said, "They seemed to be looking at me with such expectation. I felt that everyone there wanted to raise a hand, wave at me and shout, 'Look at me, look at me! I have a story, let me tell my story.' And I realized that my greatest job was just to listen and honor their stories."

I was grateful for the lesson the chaplain taught me, that everyone has a story and that the greatest service we can do is honor those stories by active listening.

Do you know someone who is eager to tell his or her story but has no one to hear it? Express your gratitude by being willing to honor that person's story, even if you've already heard it a dozen times.

—JAA

September 3

AT COFFEE THIS MORNING in a local coffee house, I was approached by a woman whose face I recognized but whose name I could not recall (at my age, this is not unusual). She introduced herself as my son Ronald's kindergarten teacher and then talked about how fondly she remembers him and how happy it makes her when she sees him doing well these days. Isn't that something? Ronald is thirty years old.

If there is a group of people on this earth for whom we should all be grateful, it is schoolteachers. They're frequently overworked, always underpaid, and rarely honored for what they do.

Do you know a schoolteacher? Express your gratitude to him or her today.

—JAA

September 4

MY FRIEND JIM NEWBY writes in his book, *Sacred Chaos*, "There is an old neighborhood in all of us—a place where we were formed and which we helped to form. The only place where it has stayed the same since leaving is in one's mind, for we know that time cannot stand still . . . but this is still home, and I could still claim it as 'My Neighborhood.'"

Is there an old neighborhood or an old home place that you still remember today with gratitude?

—JAA

September 5

MY GIRLFRIEND, JOANNE, AND I spent a fall weekend in Chicago. The weather was perfect, so we meandered through the north-side neighborhoods, walked a long stretch of the lakefront, and relaxed among tourists in the famous Millennium Park.

Joanne was interested in taking a boat cruise on the Chicago River, so we made a reservation for Sunday afternoon. I had been in Chicago many times over the years on business and for pleasure, but I had never seen the city from the water. The cruise turned out to be the highlight of the weekend.

Chicago is the city that built the first skyscraper, and it is home to some of the most impressive architecture in the world. Viewing these many building from the vantage point of the river was spectacular. It made me appreciate the architectural history of the city and the river in a new way.

Would a new perspective open your eyes to present wonders in your life?

—SJP

September 6

AT THE RIVER'S EDGE
I want to talk about things I love:
how the trees stand next to the edge
so lush and upright, patient in the wind;
the colors of small stones just underwater;
the darting of minnows and the sudden pause
as they hang like a cloud against the current;
the way the water whispers at the shore;
cradling grains of sand always, back and forth;
and the water strider, easy in his miracle,
walking anywhere, his feet dimpling the surface
so easy for all the rest of us to break.
(by Phil Hey, used with permission)

What in the natural world do you talk about with such gratitude?

—JAA

September 7

I LOVE PLYMOUTH CONGREGATIONAL Church of Des Moines. It ain't my preacher grandfather's church or my late preacher father's church, but I suspect it would be my late mother's church. She was an artist whose artistic church work was limited to painting baptisteries. They were marvelous things, invoking images of palm trees and blue waters so that the minister and the people being baptized looked as if they were waist deep in the river.

A romantic image, to be sure, and certainly not representative of the land or the river in which Jesus was baptized. But it did the job. At Plymouth, we don't baptize by immersion, which might be a relief to my mother. But we do have an art gallery, and that would have delighted her.

What church or house of worship are you grateful for today?

—JAA

CHOOSING GRATITUDE

September 8

LIKE MILLIONS OF KIDS who grew up between 1970 and 2001, our son watched *Mister Rogers' Neighborhood* almost every weekday for many years. It was popular to satirize the slow-paced, folksy mannerisms of Mister Rogers, but the impact he had on America's children and on their families is immeasurable. Generations of kids loved and trusted this caring adult who spoke directly to them in the most personal and respectful way.

Of course, moms and dads watching the program learned things, too. Many of us adopted the language Mr. Rogers used in speaking to our own children.

To me, his most powerful words were those he used to close his show each day: "I like you just the way you are."

Around our house, those words are repeated often—substituting the word "love" for "like." We try to live by them, striving to accept each other exactly the way we are.

Today, practice Mr. Rogers's motto, accepting others just the way they are and being grateful for the uniqueness of each person.

—SJP

September 9

"He is a wise man who does not grieve for the things which he has not, but rejoices for those which he has." (Epictetus)

ONCE AGAIN, WE FIND wise words from an ancient philosopher. It is clear to me that, for thousands of years, the world has been in constant need of the encouragement to live in gratitude.

Live in gratitude today, and encourage someone else to do the same.

—JAA

September 10

WHEN I FIRST MET people who described themselves as on a spiritual journey, I had to admit I wasn't sure what they were talking about. The more I got to know them and learn about what they were doing, I came to believe that a "spiritual journey" involved prayer and meditation, retreats, listening to certain kinds of music, reading the poetry of the mystics, and so on. And I participated in a lot of that over the years. Then my wife (and co-author) was elected to a high public office in our state, and I took on the role of stay-at-home husband and father. It was through that experience that I realized that my spiritual journey, my connection with the sacred, could include such unlikely things as cleaning the gutters, mowing the lawn, doing the laundry, cooking meals, shopping for groceries—in other words, everyday domestic things. I came to realize that the spiritual journey is not so much what I did but how I did the things I had to do. Was I grudging and inconvenienced, or was I joyful and grateful for the opportunity and the ability to embrace the everydayness of my life? You know the answer.

Can you embrace and be grateful for doing the chores and fulfilling the obligations of everyday life?

—JAA

September 11

I HAVE AN ACQUAINTANCE who has spent the greater part of his teaching career in special education. If you know any special education teachers, then you know the important work they do, not just for their students but for our society. Those teachers become strong advocates for their kids, and recently, my acquaintance made a special effort to give me the privilege of seeing the artwork of a young man with a severe intellectual disability. It was exquisite. The young man sits, and with only his imagination he draws and illustrates stories. He talks constantly to himself as he works, but his art speaks to everyone who sees it. I'm grateful to his teacher for making the effort to expose this art to a wider audience.

Do you know any special education teachers? If so, tell them how grateful you are for their work.

—JAA

September 12

MY SISTER, EVE, IS the former editor of a quilting magazine. She has long since retired, but she remains engaged in the culture of quilting. A few years ago, when I redecorated our family room, she graciously volunteered to make pillows for my new sofa and chairs.

When the pair of pillows arrived, imagine my pleasure in finding these quotes in the center of each beautifully quilted pillow:

A sister shares childhood memories and grown-up dreams.
Supportive sisters appreciate their differences as much as their similarities.

Today, take time to express your love and appreciation for a sibling or other family member to whom you feel close.

—SJP

September 13

"When we are no longer able to change a situation, we are challenged to change ourselves." (Viktor Frankl)

DR. FRANKL WAS A prisoner in a Nazi concentration camp. From that experience, he wrote *Man's Search for Meaning*, in which he explained the possibility of finding meaning even in the harshest circumstances. Clearly unable to change the situation, he changed the way he thought about the situation. His book has been an inspiration to me for years and has helped me find meaning in, and gratitude for, my life and my work.

Let Dr. Frankl's advice help you find meaning and gratitude in whatever you set yourself to do.

—JAA

September 14

MY WIFE NEVER THOUGHT of herself as a singer, and she does not come from a particularly musical family. As I have developed some minor vocal chord problems in the past couple of years, I've stopped singing in church. This has allowed me to do what I should have done all along: listen to Sally sing. I think I've finally convinced her that she has a lovely voice, so now I think she sings with more confidence. Not only that, but she sings on pitch, which is more than half the congregation can do. Does this mean I'm grateful that my voice problems forced me to do what I should do more of: keep my own mouth shut and listen? Yes.

Do you, as I do, have to work at listening more? Other people's voices, speaking or singing, are blessings. Let's listen.

—JAA

September 15

LIFELONG LEARNING HAS BECOME a popular phrase if not a popular pastime in recent years. It seems we're regularly being admonished to "learn something new." Well, that's easy for me. All I have to do is go to lunch with my son Rick. He is a lawyer, and one of his hobbies is the study of word origins. (In fact, the American Bar Association published his book, *Word Origins for Lawyers*.) All I have to do is ask a simple question about a word, such as, "Rick, I know the suffix 'son' as in Johnson or Richardson means 'son of,' but what does the 'mac' or 'mc,' such as in 'McKinstry' or 'MacDaniels,' mean?" His answer: the same thing. The "mac or mc prefix means 'son of.'" I've learned a lot about the evolution of the English language from Rick. The question may be, "So what? How does it help you to know those little bits of information?" Answer: It's not that I know them now but that I learned something new. It's the learning not necessarily the knowing. Of course, if I get a chance, I can always use these tidbits of knowledge at a party to make myself look a lot smarter than I am, thanks to Rick.

Be grateful for your ability to learn, and learn something new today.

—JAA

September 16

"Thankfulness brings you to the place where the Beloved lives." (Rumi)

I LEARNED ABOUT THE poetry of the Sufi mystic Rumi many years ago and have a collection of his writings. He frequently uses the term "the Beloved," which has been interpreted in several ways, one of which is God or perhaps Jesus. I would add this thought: whenever you live in gratitude, it reveals the Divine that lives within you, and when others accept the gratitude you offer, there is created yet another dwelling place for the Beloved.

Think today about the connection between gratitude and the Divine.

—JAA

September 17

SIGN SEEN ON A visit to the Delta Blues Museum: "Ain't it nice to be nice to people who are nice?"

Yes.

But that's the easy part. It's also nice, though difficult, to be nice to people who are not nice. What makes it so difficult is the realization that people who are not nice may not be nice in return. But you might be surprised; you might brighten the day of someone who doesn't expect to be treated with kindness or respect. They might even be grateful they crossed paths with you today.

Can you bring yourself to be nice to everyone today?

—JAA

September 18

I ATTENDED A RETIREMENT party for a colleague a few years ago. I'd never thought of him as eloquent until I heard his parting comments: "I have worked the last twenty-two years for a company that cares about people and expresses that concern by action. I've been part of that, so I know what success is. . . . I have not fulfilled all my objectives, my hopes, my dreams, so I know what adjustment is. . . . And because I have known all these things, I truly know contentment."

It struck me that too many of us are focused on success and upward movement, and too few of us are grateful for the great gift of contentment.

Are you content to be who you are and to do what you do? Are you grateful for that?

—JAA

September 19

WHEN OUR SON RONALD was first diagnosed with autism, it was a terrible blow. We tried to learn everything we could about it. We went to doctors of various sorts. We even took him to psychic healers. We were looking for a miracle, of course. At some point after a few years, I finally recognized the real miracle workers and realized that miracles were happening every day, one person at a time, one teacher, one friend, one family member, one coach, one music teacher, one ranch-hand wrangler, and one parent at a time. I also realized that Ronald himself is the biggest miracle of all.

Who in your life is a living miracle for whom you feel grateful today?

—JAA

September 20

THERE WERE DAYS I thought I wouldn't be able to afford to stay in college. I worked a couple of jobs but still was short of money and had to skip meals to make ends almost meet. But people helped me. The dean of students talked to the bank and arranged a loan; a local businessman gave me odd jobs in addition to the other work. I was fortunate and made it through. I am not wealthy, but several years ago, I was able to make a small endowment for scholarships at my alma mater, designated for students in need of financial support. Over the years, I have received letters of appreciation from students who are benefitting from the endowment. I am grateful that I was able to help in their education, and I am grateful beyond words for those letters.

Is there a way that you can help or encourage some young person in getting a good education?

—JAA

September 21

"There are only two ways to live your life. One is as though nothing is a miracle. The other is as though everything is a miracle." (Albert Einstein)

I USED TO WANT miracles, but they were more often than not material miracles: more money, a big car, and so on. As I got older and the realities of life closed in, I wanted my brother's cancer to be cured, my son's autism to be cured, and so on. I was disappointed that none of that happened, or so I thought. My brother lived two and a half good years after the diagnosis, and he and I had many good times. My son graduated from a two-year college course for people with intellectual disabilities, has a good job, has his own apartment—plus a dog, friends, and a wonderful girlfriend. My problem in wanting the miracles was that I was not recognizing the miracles that were already there. This doesn't mean I don't still miss my brother or that I don't still wish for more progress by my son; it only means that by trying to live a life of gratitude, I realize that every blessing I count is, in fact, a miracle.

Try counting your own miracles today.

—JAA

September 22

"IT'S GOOD TO BE just plain happy; it's a little better to know that you're happy, but to understand that you're happy and to know why and how . . . and still be happy, be happy in the being and the knowing, well that is beyond happiness, that is bliss." Henry Miller said this in 1941. And it's worth saying again and again.

Be beyond happy today; be blissful and be grateful for it.

—JAA

CHOOSING GRATITUDE

September 23

WITH ALL THE TALK about education reform, I worry that we put so much emphasis on training our children to be workers that we lose sight of training them to be good people and thus good citizens. In fact, in the final two decades of the twentieth century, we in America became good at teaching our children only the little virtues, when in the words of Natalia Ginzburg, they "should be taught not the little virtues but the great ones. Not thrift but generosity . . . not caution but courage . . . not shrewdness but frankness and a love of truth . . . ." And of course I would add "gratitude."

Make a commitment today to let your life of gratitude demonstrate not the little virtues but the great ones.

—JAA

September 24

I HEARD THE NEWS last week that Burl Armstrong, an old high school classmate, had died. Another classmate got in touch to ask if I remembered him. I did more than that: Burl had a role in changing my life years ago. He was in the school band and persuaded me to join, even though I did not yet play an instrument. But I taught myself the clarinet, with coaching from teachers, and as a result, years later, I received a band scholarship to college. That experience, in turn, introduced me to the world of classical music, which continues to enrich my life today. Thus, it is with affection and deep gratitude that I do, indeed, remember Burl.

Has there been someone in your life who helped you in a way that has lasted until now? If you can be in touch with that person, express your gratitude today.

—JAA

September 25

IF YOU READ THE entry for September 11, you read about the remarkable artwork of a special education student. Because my wife and I have been active with disability rights over the years, we always try to respond when someone calls our attention to something like that artwork.

We were so impressed that we are helping to arrange a showing of it at a gallery in our church. I'm told that the special education class will do a "field trip" to view the art when it is hung. Gratitude? Oh yes, for the young man, for the artwork, for the teachers who give extra time and effort to make a difference.

Do you know teachers and others who go the extra mile to help someone who can't help himself? Be very grateful for those people.

—JAA

September 26

I CAME ACROSS A PIECE of writing that is encouraging to people of all ages, but particularly to those who can see life's deadline looming: "Whether seventy or seventeen there is in every being's heart the love of wonder, the sweet amazement of the stars . . . the undaunted challenge of events, the unfailing child-like appetite for what is next, and the joy of the game of life. You are as young as your faith, as old as your doubt; as young as your self-confidence, as old as your fear; as young as your hope, as old as your despair." (author unknown)

Be grateful today for the "joy of the game of life."

—JAA

September 27

"Work hard, but give time to your love, family, and friends. Because when we die, nobody will remember presentations, meetings, degrees, and overtime." (Anonymous)

I SUSPECT THAT WHOEVER wrote this must have spent a lot of time on the job and then one day asked himself or herself, "Why am I working myself to the point that I don't get to focus on the people I love?" I asked myself that question many years ago. It was not that I didn't love my job; I did, but it was a different kind of love in that I loved the job, but, unlike loved ones, the job didn't love me back. It took a while, but I made the changes that put me in sync with this quote. I worked hard (still do), but I don't let it take time away from loved ones, and I take time to count my blessings and be grateful every day.

Are you able to keep the job, or other activities, in perspective and to balance your life between work and loved ones? Living in gratitude will help you do so.

—JAA

September 28

GOVERNMENT TAKES A LOT of criticism these days, some of it well founded, some of it nonsense. I want to say a word on behalf of two programs for which I am grateful, the National Endowment for the Arts and the National Endowment for the Humanities. Our communities, large and small, have been enriched by the local talent these two programs support. Arts organizations, from orchestras to writing workshops, have multiplied in the years of the two "endowments." And I suspect many of us are not even aware of how much impact they have had on our lives and communities.

Take time today to be grateful for our two splendid "endowments."

—JAA

September 29

MUSIC IS CENTRAL TO the experience at our church's Saturday night worship service. We have a seven-piece band and two talented vocalists. Some nights the place really rocks with everything from old-time spirituals to Beatles songs. The service attracts a diverse and loyal crowd.

Occasionally, one or two young children will break into spontaneous dancing and prancing in the area in front of the band. One lively evening, the bandleader issued an invitation to dance, and almost immediately a couple of preschoolers were on their feet, followed soon by a mentally challenged forty-year-old man waving his hands and smiling happily. The scene felt awkward, but only for a moment, because then a woman rose from her seat, joined the man on the floor, and began swinging and swaying joyfully to the music.

It struck me as such a moment of grace. I am grateful that this woman knew instinctively what to do. She acted on behalf of the community, demonstrating how to respond inclusively and with our hearts. I don't remember what the sermon was that evening, but I will always remember this lesson in love.

Are you grateful for those who teach, by example, the real meaning of community?

—SJP

September 30

MANY YEARS AGO, I was a reluctant homeowner. It seemed to me that all my home-owning friends spent most of their weekends in hard labor, plus spent a lot of money on everything from hammers to lawn mowers, not to mention hoses, sprinklers, hedge trimmers, and so on. Of course, home is more than a house, and there are millions of people who create a home for themselves and their families regardless of the structure itself. Still, I am now so grateful to have a house and home that you couldn't bribe me to live in an apartment. As for the cost, Samuel Johnson once said, "No money is better spent than what is laid out for domestic satisfaction." Domestic satisfaction. That's a good way to describe it, and so what if I can't drive past the hardware store without buying something for the home?

No matter whether you have a mansion or live in an efficiency apartment, join me today in being grateful for home.

—JAA

October 1

WE LIVE IN AN impatient world. I sometimes think that the shortest measurement of time is the interval between when the light turns green and someone behind me honks the horn. We may be the most in-a-hurry people in history, but you and I don't have to give in to the world's mad rush. Almost by definition, a life of gratitude encompasses the virtue of thoughtful patience. Put another way, we can't feel and express gratitude in a hurry. We have to slow down, turn off the cell phones, turn off the TV, put the computer to sleep, and simply be quiet and relax.

Here's what others have written about the virtue of patience:

"Have patience. All things are difficult before they become easy." (Saadi)

"How poor are those that have not patience! What wound did ever heal but by degree?" (Shakespeare)

"Have patience with all things, but, first of all with yourself." (St. Francis de Sales)

"Patience is the best remedy for every trouble." (Titus Maccius Plautus)

If you are a patient person, be grateful for that; if not, write down the ways or situations in which you can work to be more patient, thus more grateful.

—JAA

October 2

MY HUSBAND AND I are blessed with the good fortune to have close friends who are foodies of the first order. Their kitchen is the heart of their home and lives. Cooking and serving good—*really good*—food is the way they express themselves, and they are lavish in their hospitality to family, friends, and new acquaintances.

A meal in their home is a sumptuous feast for the senses. The foods are always of the highest quality and freshest ingredients, and loving attention is paid to the preparation and presentation of every plate and platter. Yet everything feels relaxed, unpretentious, and welcoming. Theirs is a table where there is always room for more guests, always an abundance of food to share, and always a feeling of affection and goodwill. If it sounds a lot like heaven, maybe it is.

Are you grateful for the simple acts of gracious hospitality in your life? Are you able to create opportunities for food and fellowship with others?

—SJP

October 3

"One of the oldest human needs is having someone to wonder where you are when you don't come home at night." (Margaret Mead)

AND I WOULD ADD that it's just as important a human need for that someone who is wondering about you to know when you get home safely. I write as someone who tends to be a worrier. Our son Ronald is almost thirty, and despite his autism, or perhaps because of it, he is always reliable in letting his mother and me know where he is and when he is back at his apartment. I'm not sure how he became so imbued with that impulse to keep us informed, but I am intensely grateful that he does.

Be grateful for that someone who, out of love, always wants to be sure you are safe.

—JAA

October 4

YEARS AGO, AFTER I complimented him on his cornbread, my friend Sam Gore sent me the recipe. At the time, he was a captain with the now-defunct Eastern Airlines, so the recipe arrived handwritten on the back of an Eastern ticket folder. Also, it was written in the vernacular of the Southern backcountry folks we'd both grown up with.

First thing is, check to be sure that there ain't nobody coming to eat that you don't particlly like 'cause hit would be a shame for them to git aholt of any of this cornbread.

Ingredients:
meal (stone ground, self-risin'), egg, lard, buttermilk, salt, skillet (iron)

Directions:
Put the lard in the skillet and put it in a hot stove, and while it is gittin' good and hot, mix the meal and salt and the eggs and pour in enough buttermilk to make it kind of sloppy. Then pour in the hot lard and stir it up good and pour it back into the hot skillet. Bake at 475 degrees; when cornbread is about done, brown the top some under the broiler. Hope you remember to take the butter out to soften at the start of all this.

This is the first time I've shared Sam's light-hearted recipe. Try it yourself. You'll be grateful that you did.

—JAA

CHOOSING GRATITUDE

October 5

A FRIEND OF THE family called me yesterday. Dorothy is actually my parents' contemporary and friend. When I was growing up, she and her husband, Dick, and their kids were very close to our family. We spent many summers together at their lakeside cabin, and they joined us every fall for the opening of pheasant hunting season.

Dorothy lives alone now in Tallahassee, Dick having passed away several years ago. She has called me only a handful of times in the past twenty years, but each time it takes me by surprise and opens up a cascade of wonderful memories.

She asks about my parents and their health—seeming relieved to know that they are still getting along well. I ask about her three boys, at one time special in my life, but now, fifty years later, nearly strangers.

I check to be sure she has my parents' phone number—she does. And then we say our good-byes. My day feels brightened by this call from out of the past, and I vow to return the favor in the future.

Is there someone from your childhood who would be grateful to hear from you?

—SJP

October 6

"Man is fond of counting his troubles, but he does not count his joys. If he counted them up as he ought to, he would see that every lot has enough happiness provided for it." (Fyodor Dostoevsky)

THIS IS ANOTHER WAY of reminding us to focus less on our troubles and more on our blessings and joys. If we do that, gratitude naturally fills our lives.

Put your troubles in the background today and concentrate on your joys.

—JAA

October 7

ON THE HIGHWAY NEAR Albion, Iowa, is a house that is so much like a house I used to drive by when I was in the Air Force in France that I catch my breath when I see it. I am immediately transported by memory back to that French highway and to those years. The same kind of mental time travel happens when I hear certain music or smell certain aromas. For instance, the smell of wood smoke on a damp fall morning takes me back to my family's home in Mississippi. I don't mean to say that I long to be back in those times or places, but I do smile at some of the memories, and I am grateful that I have them.

What stimulates your memories today?

—JAA

October 8

"It may be that the satisfaction I need depends on my going away, so that when I've gone and come back, I'll find it at home." (Rumi)

WHEN I WAS YOUNG, I could not wait to travel. Like a lot of other young people, I was eager to see what was "out there." Surely it would be better, more interesting, more intriguing, and in every way more compelling than where I was living and what I was doing. I did get to travel; the Air Force sent me to France, from where I visited most of the rest of Europe. Temporary duty took me to Libya and Morocco among other places. I thought I was living the good and exciting life, and in many ways I was, but I always felt that it was temporary, that it wouldn't satisfy me in the long term. More and more, I wanted to return to civilian life, get a good job, and settle down. This of course is what I did. It has not been as exciting as flying jet fighters, but for me it has deeper and more enduring rewards that are sources of gratitude every day.

Look around you today. Have you found satisfaction right where you are?

—JAA

CHOOSING GRATITUDE

October 9

ALCOHOLICS ANONYMOUS IS A wonderful organization. I know there are those who criticize it, but I've witnessed its work with friends and in my own family, and I don't understand the criticisms. There are lessons for all of us in its twelve steps. One of them is about making amends. I've been told that this is one of the hardest steps of all because it involves contacting the people—friends, loved ones—whose lives have been affected negatively by the alcoholic's actions, then apologizing, asking forgiveness, and otherwise trying to rectify the damage. I have participated in Al-Anon, the parallel program for loved ones, and all I can say is that I am grateful beyond describing for AA.

Are you grateful for AA, a church, or another service organization that has helped you, a friend, or a loved one?

—JAA

October 10

MY HUSBAND MAY NOT have invented the saying, "A place for everything and everything in its place," but he lives by it, and he thinks other people should, too.

His obsessive habit of keeping everything in a particular location and returning it to that location can be useful, and I often benefit from his tidiness. But on occasion, our different tolerance levels for "out-of-place" objects can cause minor skirmishes. Fortunately, over the years, we have learned to use humor to deal with what otherwise might lead to accusations and arguments. I appreciate my partner's willingness to accept our differences and to defuse potential conflicts with a smile. And I am grateful for the wisdom and maturity that a good marriage instills.

Are you grateful for the ways in which you are challenged to accept the things in your spouse or friend that are fundamentally different from you?

—SJP

October 11

I'M GRATEFUL THAT I found a scrapbook of poems written by my father years ago. Here's one:

Eternity
I behold Life's golden sunset,
O'er the mystic hills of Time;
And I wait me in the twilight
For the evening bells to chime.
Soon they'll chime from out the shadows,
That are falling over me;
And I'll knock upon the portals,
Of a grand Eternity.
(From a 1939 church bulletin, written by my minister father)

Are there scrapbooks and old albums that could be a source of gratitude for you today? Why not look for them now?

—JAA

October 12

I USED TO BE drawn to contemporary architecture and thought I'd want a very contemporary house someday. But when I see all the restoration and preservation work being done to resurrect the beauty of older homes, I no longer am attracted to the clean, uncluttered lines of the contemporary. I still appreciate the design itself, but I don't want to live with it every day. I am grateful for the dedication and talent of the preservationists who look at something old and declining and see instead its potential for new life.

Be grateful today for the designers, architects, and builders who create our places of everyday comfort, regardless of the style.

—JAA

October 13

THE NATURE OF LIFE seems to be that, despite how much effort we put into our work or how fervently we strive to keep our spirits up, there inevitably come those "down" times. I don't mean clinical depression—only disappointment in something we've done or failed to do. It happens to me infrequently but regularly. That's when I turn to my wife or friends for a boost.

Albert Schweitzer wrote this: "At times our own light goes out and is rekindled by a spark from another person. Each of us has cause to think with deep gratitude of those who have lighted the flame within us."

Be grateful if you have a friend or loved one to whom you can turn when you need a spark to rekindle your light.

—JAA

October 14

MOST OF THE YOUNG people I know do not wear wristwatches; if they want to know the time, they look at their cell phones. Not me. I not only wear a wristwatch and have clocks in every room but also have a grandfather clock. My son collects cuckoo clocks; he has five. There is something celebratory about marking the passage of time with chiming and cuckooing, almost like shouting, "Hear Ye, Hear Ye, another hour has passed, and all is well." Or to put it another way, the chiming and cuckooing reminds us to pause and be grateful for this minute, this hour, this day.

Do you have ways to remind yourself to be grateful for this minute, this hour, this day?

—JAA

October 15

A FRAMED CROSS-STITCH hangs on the wall in my parents' house. It reads,

1. Don't let little people make you small.
2. Get up, get dressed, and if you still feel bad, go back to bed.
3. Life is NO bowl of cherries.
4. You are your own worst enemy.
5. There's nothing like looking, if you want to find something.

My sister, Eve, created the framed wall hanging for our mother's seventieth birthday. It is a collection of sayings that each of Mom's five children recall as "words to live by."

None of these were written down before Eve asked us each to recall "advice" we remembered from our childhood. I consider them practical wisdoms, tinged with humor, and they are embedded in each of us in ways of which we are probably not fully aware. I have passed on at least some of them to my own son.

It's nice to have them recorded—especially in embroidery.

Can you recall things your parents told you that may now hold special wisdom and value? Write them down and share them with a sibling or other relative. You may find something surprising to appreciate.

—SJP

October 16

"Drop the question what tomorrow will bring, and count as profit every day fate allows you." (Horace)

THE BUDDHISTS ENCOURAGE THE concept of "nowness," that is, living in the present moment. Easier said than done, of course, because we are always reflecting on, or worrying about, the past and always planning, or dreading, the future. I think the best rule is to learn from the past, plan for the future, but live in the present. We can begin to do that by simply sitting silently or meditating or praying, and counting today's blessings with gratitude.

Try it today. Focus on gratitude for now and put the past and the future out of your mind.

—JAA

October 17

GEORGE BERNARD SHAW SAID, "I am of the opinion that my life belongs to the community, and as long as I live, it is my privilege to do for it whatever I can."

We are in all kinds of communities, and we should be grateful for each of them. There are of course the neighborhood and the city or town. Our churches are communities of faith but also communities of friendship. When some of us gather regularly for coffee, we create a little community in the coffee shop. There are communities at work and other communities at clubs. When we travel in a group, or even take a cruise with strangers, we create temporary communities. It's clear that we are naturally drawn to communities as places of nurture and comfort and support for one another.

List the communities in which you participate, and be grateful for all of them today.

—JAA

October 18

He drew a circle
That shut me out
Heretic, rebel,
A thing to flout.

But, love and I
Had the wit to win,
We drew a circle
That took him in.

(Attributed to Edwin Markham)

I LEARNED THAT VERSE in Sunday school many, many years ago. I memorized very few poems in my childhood, but that one stuck with me. It is a simple but profound philosophy.

Be grateful for the circles that draw you in, and work to create circles that drawn in others.

—SJP

October 19

IN MY WORK WITH mediation and conflict resolution, there are two major tools: time and patience. These, of course, are themselves in conflict with the way our world seems to work these days. Many of the people I've worked with insist that we "get this over with" or that we set a deadline for resolution. I like to ask, "Do we not have time for peacemaking?" because conflict resolution and mediation are about nothing more than peace making. After that comes agreement about the issues and next steps.

Some of my more gratifying experiences have been bringing people together toward a common goal or understanding.

If you feel in conflict with someone today, take the first step toward peacemaking. You'll be grateful you did.

—JAA

October 20

"Be content with what you have; rejoice in the way things are. When you realize there is nothing lacking, the whole worlds belongs to you." (Lao Tzu)

THERE IS MUCH TO be gained from overcoming the psychology of scarcity that makes us believe there's not enough and we'd better get ours. Lao Tzu is describing the psychology of abundance and telling us that what we have is enough. The challenge is to believe it and to be grateful for it.

Do you believe that what you have is enough, and are you grateful for that?

—JAA

October 21

"How wonderful it is that nobody need wait a single moment before starting to improve the world." (Anne Frank)

THERE SEEMS TO BE so much to improve in this world that the prospect of trying to do it can become overwhelming. How do we change the world? First, by realizing that if we improve anything, even ourselves, we have changed the world because the world will not be the same was it was before.

Today, embrace the opportunity to improve the world.

—SJP

October 22

TOM VILSACK, FORMER GOVERNOR of Iowa and now US Secretary of Agriculture, found inspiration in this famous quote. He shared it widely and had it done in calligraphy for friends. I have a copy in my office as a daily reminder to ignore the critics and never fear failure.

> It is not the critic who counts, not the man who points out how the strong man stumbled, or where the doer of deeds could have done them better. The credit belongs to the man who is actually in the arena; whose face is marred by dust and sweat and blood; who strives valiantly; who errs and comes short again and again, who knows the great enthusiasms, the great devotions, and spends himself in a worthy cause; who, at the best, knows the triumph of high achievement, and who, at the worst if he fails, at least fails while daring greatly, so that his place shall never be with those cold and timid souls who know neither victory nor defeat. (Theodore Roosevelt)

Are you grateful for the things you have learned through failure as well as success?

—SJP

October 23

I INTERVIEWED A MAN a few years ago about his church work. He said this: "I feel that seeking social justice through the church is a spiritual expression. However you do it, if you help people find meaning in their lives, then you'll find meaning in your own life. And it doesn't matter whether you're old or young, retired or still working."

Let's be grateful today for those who find meaning in their own lives by helping other people find meaning in theirs.

—JAA

CHOOSING GRATITUDE

October 24

I GET A LITTLE discouraged about how poetry is viewed in our society. Why? Because, despite how much poetry is being published these days, I find that many people say they don't read poetry at all. Their reasons seem to have to do with the poetry they read in school. They didn't like it then, and they figure they won't like it now. I try to explain that the essence of poetry is not only what the words say but also what lies beneath the words—that what the words inspire or provoke in the reader is also part of the poetry.

T. S. Eliot said that "genuine poetry can communicate before it is understood." I think it is true that poetry has a mystical quality that speaks to the soul rather than to the intellect. And I am grateful for that.

Read a poem today, and let it feed your soul.

—JAA

October 25

A DEAR FRIEND WHO has suffered for years with severe neck and back pain just came through a successful but complicated surgery. He reports that he is now pain free. There are so many complaints these days about our health care system that they tend to drown out the gratitude expressed by people like my friend, people who have been relieved of difficult and frightening physical problems—to put it another way, people who know firsthand the blessing of good health and medical care.

Think with gratitude about the friends and loved ones whose lives have been made better by health practitioners.

—JAA

October 26

I'M ALWAYS HAPPY WHEN, at the end of winter, the first green shoots of my early daffodils begin to peek out of the ground, often through the snow. I'm always happy when, at the end of a season of weeding and yard work, the first killing frost comes and tinges everything in white. I'm always happy when, after raking leaves, taking in plants, and putting away equipment, the first snow falls. It's not that I'm happy all the time, but I am grateful for both the beginning and end of each season, that most ancient way of measuring the years.

Be grateful today for the earth's changes that symbolize to us the cycles of life.

—JAA

October 27

"We can only be said to be alive in those moments when our hearts are conscious of our treasures." (Thornton Wilder)

I WORK HARD AT being conscious of my treasures. To put it another way, I count my blessings every day, partly as a way of celebrating my life and, to be honest, partly as a way of fending off all the negative stuff that can permeate my consciousness if I let the world be too much with me. After all, being happy and living in gratitude are largely matters of choice.

Make your own choice today to be happy, count your blessings, and live in gratitude.

—JAA

October 28

Time comes with kind oblivious shade
And daily darker sets it
And if no more mistakes you've made
Time soon forgets it.

MY MOTHER SAW THIS poem engraved on a building as she stepped off a train in the 1940s. She said it spoke to her as she was dealing with the shame and guilt of unwed motherhood. She shared this with me over thirty-two years ago during some tumultuous times in my life, when I was coping with my own shame and guilt over infidelity and divorce.

I kept the poem pinned to my bulletin board for many years. The yellow aging slip of paper, ragged at the edges, now rests inside the front cover of my desktop dictionary.

I am grateful for my mother's wisdom and her willingness to be vulnerable by sharing her personal story with me.

—SJP

October 29

A ZEN MASTER IS QUOTED as saying, "Everything is perfect, but there's still room for improvement." I puzzled over this a bit until I realized that everything doesn't have to be perfect for us to be happy— far from it, in fact. We just have to accept the imperfections; we can even be grateful for them and not let them dominate our lives or our spirits.

Can you be grateful for the imperfections in your life?

—JAA

October 30

THERE IS A LOT of complaining about digital technology and particularly about young people's obsession with it. Yes, it can be irritating to see a gathering of teenagers who, while they are in a face-to-face group, are busily texting someone else somewhere else. But there's another side to this story. We who are involved with people with disabilities might call cell phones "assistive technology." No, cell phones are not one of the wonderful technologies that aid in moving or hearing or seeing or speaking, or in cognitive ability, but they do assist in the quality of life for some people with disabilities. Our son with autism, for instance, stays in touch with friends and family by calling, texting, sending photos, and so on. Of course, his cell phone is something of a lifeline to his parents. He calls with any number of concerns, most of them fairly insignificant to me but very important to him. I am grateful for the technology that lets us be in touch, whether his mother and I are home or on vacation in a foreign country. And I admit I'm still impressed that he can dial my cell number and my phone will ring no matter where I am. It's a comfort to both of us. In fact, I call it assistive technology for both of us.

Are there technologies that make your life, or the life of a loved one, somehow better? Let's all be grateful for these sometimes irritating, but always extraordinary machines.

—JAA

October 31

WE CAN EXPRESS LOVE in many ways. I thought of this at the air-port, of all places, where I noticed a young adult woman with an obvious intellectual disability who was being guided across the busy street by an older man whom I took to be her father. She jumped at the sounds of the traffic, her eyes widened with fear, and she glanced anxiously at the man who held her arm and spoke calmly, looking at her as if in normal conversation, as if nothing else was happening, as if just crossing the street with her was the most important thing in the world. And of course, for both of them, it was.

I was very moved with gratitude by this everyday tableau. Whoever said "Love conquers all" had it right.

What calm, reassuring people in your life are you grateful for?

—JAA

November 1

BEGIN THIS MONTH BY thinking about generosity. If you live in gratitude, you will naturally be a more generous person—generous with your attention, generous with your support for others, and generous with your material resources.

Confucius considered generosity to be one of the five things that constitutes perfect virtue.

Here are some of the many other words devoted to generosity:

"Great wisdom is generous . . . ." (Chuang-tzu)

"You will make all kinds of mistakes; but as long as you are generous and true, and also fierce, you cannot hurt the world or even seriously distress her." (Winston Churchill)

"You have not lived until you have done something for someone who cannot repay you." (John Bunyan)

"The value of a man resides in what he gives and not in what he is capable of receiving." (Albert Einstein)

Take time today to identify and write down your opportunities to be generous.

—JAA

November 2

MY SON'S EVERYDAY LIFE experiences are a constant reminder of the goodness in the world.

An acquaintance told me about an instance she observed at a Barnes & Noble bookstore where Ronald was shopping with a friend. He had just reached the front of the line with a couple of CDs in hand, which he had carefully selected. It was then that he discovered he didn't have enough money to pay for them. Like many people with a cognitive disability, he found the disappointment and disruption in plans too much to handle. He was visibly upset.

A man in line behind Ronald saw his distress and quietly stepped up to help. The stranger took out his wallet, handed the store clerk a twenty-dollar bill, and the transaction was promptly completed. I doubt that Ronald knew enough even to thank his rescuer, but I hope the gentleman knows how much his good deed was appreciated.

Have you witnessed or experienced the kindness of a stranger? Are you grateful to those who help someone in need?

—SJP

November 3

MY FRIEND JEANNE CAHILL sent me this story of gratitude, double gratitude in fact.

> Rescued from an abusive home, she was skittish, refused eye contact and trusted no one upon arrival. The gratitude of this pit bull/ German shepherd mix is palpable. She demonstrates it with her alert brown eyes following our every move as she stations herself beside my 100-year-old husband, as though she senses his need for protection. I know she is grateful and I know he is grateful, but I think I am most grateful of all.

Do you have a pet for which you feel this kind of gratitude?

—JAA

November 4

WHEN MY FRIEND CHRISTIE VILSACK ran for Congress against an entrenched incumbent in a decidedly conservative district, she knew that the odds of winning were not good. So she outlined ten things she wanted to accomplish in her campaign that weren't dependent on defeating her opponent.

I was with her on election night, along with hundreds of her loyal supporters. Once the election outcome was clear, she gracefully conceded the race and congratulated the winner with dignity and style.

At lunch the next day, we talked about the hard-fought campaign, and she expressed genuine gratitude for the experience of running for high public office in the state she so loves. And then she pulled out the list of goals she had wanted to accomplish through her campaign and proudly checked off each one. She may not have won the race, but she was no loser.

Be grateful if you are able to define success on your own terms.

—SJP

November 5

"This life is not for complaint, but for satisfaction." (Henry David Thoreau)

AND, I MIGHT ADD, for gratitude, which derives from a deep satisfaction with life.

Make a gratitude inventory today of those things that give you satisfaction.

—JAA

November 6

I FOUND AN OLD, humorous birthday card from my son Jimmy today. I don't know the date, but I do know that it came during the years he was struggling with addiction. Written inside the card was this: "Dear Dad, Thank you for all your love and support. Looking forward to the rest of our lives together. Love, Your son, Jim." I was grateful for the message then, and I'm even more grateful today.

Is there someone in your life who has won the fight with drugs, illness, or personal trauma of one kind or another? Today is a good time to be grateful for that person's struggle and victory.

—JAA

November 7

THERE WAS MUCH TALK of eternity in the churches of my childhood. Here is what I believe now about eternity: If we can think of eternity as having already begun—and I do—and if we can find ways to be still and be open to the feast of beauty already here for us— and I try every day—and if we believe that God is part of everything in this world—and I do—then we have but to recognize that there's no waiting for eternity. I'm grateful that we can "dwell in paradise" right now, every day, every minute, as we live through this phase of eternity.

Does the thought of eternity fill you with dread of what is to come or grat-itude for what already is?

—JAA

November 8

"We are all formed of frailty and error; let us pardon reciprocally each other's folly—that is the first law of nature." (Voltaire)

THIS QUOTE IS GOOD advice for almost any human relationship: marriage, friendship, parenting, and even organizational life. Indeed, we are all capable of "folly," of dumb mistakes, of unintentional insults, or generally insensitive words or acts. Before we judge other people of those same faults, we should take Voltaire's advice and be forgiving. The ability and inclination to forgive is a dependable virtue of someone who tries to live a life of gratitude.

Does your sense of gratitude inspire you to also be a nonjudgmental and forgiving person?

—JAA

November 9

BEING PRACTICAL CAN BE a virtue, but not always.

Recently, a dinner guest let me know that she was planning to bring me flowers. My automatic response was to tell her that wasn't necessary—she didn't need to bring anything.

Through Facebook channels, I learned she was hurt that I denied her the pleasure of being nice.

I hadn't thought about it in those terms. I suppose most of us never really need the things that others give to us, but now I understand that the giving itself is the gift.

Do you gracefully accept the gratitude and generosity of others?

—SJP

November 10

MY WIFE AND I have been taking a beginning French class. I've often read that a good way to "exercise" the aging brain is to learn another language. I'm grateful that now, when I've decided to do it, I still have the mental capacity for it (I think).

Be grateful today for whatever you have the strength and mental agility to do.

—JAA

November 11

THERE WAS A STORY in the paper recently about a combat veteran who had lost arms and legs in an explosion. We've seen these stories, but this man's attitude and that of his fiancée were inspiring beyond what most of us could ever expect, and I suspect beyond what most of us would be able to do. I was deeply moved by their dignity and forbearance. Aristotle said that the ideal man bears these kinds of misfortunes "with dignity and grace, making the best of circumstances."

I am grateful, of course, for this veteran's service, but I'm grateful also for the example he sets for all of us who often are disturbed by the truly minor irritations of life.

If you face minor irritations today, be grateful for the dignified example of this wounded warrior.

—JAA

November 12

SEVERAL YEARS AGO, MY beloved uncle, my mother's brother, died. He was my hero in my growing-up years. After the divorce of my parents, he became like a surrogate father. I idolized him, and even more so when he went into the signal corps in World War II. After seeing action in New Guinea, he returned to a quiet life as a telephone lineman. He taught me to drive, loaned me his car, and helped me in myriad ways, all the while raising his own family and caring for his aged mother. Of course, he was one of many quietly heroic World War II veterans whom we have in recent years begun to honor, even though there's no way to do it adequately.

His family arranged a military funeral. Three enlisted people from the National Guard showed up in full dress uniform, two pallbearers and one bugler. I was moved by their dignity and attention to their sad and serious purpose. After the bugler played "Taps," two of the soldiers took the American flag from the coffin and, in synchronized movements, folded it. The senior soldier knelt at my aunt's chair and presented the flag "from a grateful nation." To my astonishment, there were tears rolling down his cheeks.

This simple ceremony took place in a suburban cemetery in Tennessee, not in Arlington National Cemetery. But it could not have been more meaningful in any setting.

And I could not have felt more gratitude than I did right there and then.

Please think with gratitude today of those who provide these thousands of important and dignified rituals.

—JAA

CHOOSING GRATITUDE

November 13

THE WIFE OF A World War II veteran wrote to me recently to tell about her husband's memories of coming home. He was on a hospital ship just before the end of the war, headed to a hospital for treatment of his wounds. As the ship was about to pass under the Golden Gate Bridge, he and his comrades looked up to see a huge sign saying, "A grateful nation welcomes you home." He told his wife that there was not a dry eye on the ship. And I don't have dry eyes as I write this now.

There's no end to the gratitude we owe our veterans. If you know a veteran, express your gratitude to him or her today.

—JAA

November 14

MY YOUNGER BROTHER WAS downsized out of a job late last year. He is fifty-nine years old, so his prospects for finding employment didn't seem promising.

Yet he and his wife simply put their heads down and began the challenging task of searching and applying for work in his field. And they have been amazingly successful. In the months since he lost his job, he has had contract work for all but a few weeks.

I have been in awe of his quiet confidence and determination. Despite worries about health insurance and maintaining assets, he and his wife manage their anxieties and go about life with an upbeat and optimistic attitude.

Their response to what could have been a tragedy that took them in a downward spiral has instead demonstrated their resilience.

Are you inspired by someone who has shown grace in the face of adversity?

—SJP

November 15

AS A YOUNG MAN in church and Sunday school, I heard the word "repent" used over and over, but I never asked what it really means, theologically or otherwise. One of the ministers at our church pointed out that one of the dictionary definitions is "to change one's mind" or "to change one's viewpoint." Another is to "turn around." I prefer those definitions to the one about feeling remorse over one's wrongdoings. We don't have to be burdened by guilt in order to change our attitudes or viewpoints and perhaps find a clearer, fresher way of looking at the world, at a social problem, or at a complex personal situation.

Try turning around and finding a fresh viewpoint today. It could reveal something for which you'll be very grateful.

—JAA

November 16

A BIG SNOW IS coming in this evening, so I have replenished the bird feeders with a mixture of seeds and have hung two suet cakes. Whatever this storm may bring, I know that "my" birds will be there tomorrow morning: at least sixteen cardinals, two pairs of blue jays, flickers, downy woodpeckers, purple finches, goldfinches (though not gold this time of year), nuthatches, juncos (appropriately nicknamed "snowbirds"), and plenty of sparrows.

I'm amazed at how they appear after the heaviest snows and the coldest weather, always eager for a place at the feeder. And they seem so joyful that it makes me wonder why all the other songbirds go south for the winter.

If you're even a casual birdwatcher, name the birds that make you grateful today.

—JAA

November 17

"Give thanks for unknown blessings already on their way." (Native American prayer)

MANY WRITERS AND PHILOSOPHERS have observed that the only prayer we need is "Thank you." Being aware of your blessings is the essence of gratitude.

Count your blessings again today and say, "Thank You."

—JAA

November 18

"Because one believes in oneself, one doesn't try to convince others. Because one is content with oneself, one doesn't need others' approval. Because one accepts oneself, the whole world accepts him or her." (Lao Tzu)

IT SEEMS THAT COMPETITION is built into our society. It permeates virtually every interest and activity, from simple games to sports to organizational life, and leads us to classify the participants as either winners or losers. As a kid, I was definitely among the "losers." My mother and I were poor; we lived in a federal housing project ("the projects"), and I was inept at sports, which definitely put me in the loser column at school. Still, I was brought up to believe that I could do "whatever you set your head to do" (my grandmother's words). The road to self-acceptance was bumpy and curvy for me—still is sometimes—but with the help of loved ones, I haven't run off the road. I am grateful for those loved ones, and I am determined to help others in their quest of self-acceptance and self-esteem.

In gratitude for your acceptance and approval of yourself, be a supportive resource in someone else's journey.

—JAA

November 19

"May we be strengthened with the understanding that being blessed does not mean that we shall always be spared all the disappointments and difficulties of life." (Heber J. Grant)

MY OLDER BROTHER RONALD was such a source of happiness for me that when he died, I grieved for a long time. I had many blessings at the time, but still I fell into periods of sadness because of that hole in my life. I remember wondering how I could ever feel fully blessed and happy while at the same time bearing this dreadful loss. I was advised to "work through my grief," as if the grief were just an episode and would then be gone. That seemed wrong on the face of it. Slowly, while focusing on the people I loved and was still grateful for, I sought to understand grief. Finally, it was through reading spiritual and mystical literature that I came to realize I could feel grief and joy at the same time and could be blessed and feel grateful for the gift of life's full range of emotions.

Today, can you accept all of life's disappointments and still feel blessed?

—JAA

November 20

THERE'S ALWAYS THE QUESTION, "How do I live in gratitude?" Thomas Aquinas offered this answer centuries ago: "Gratitude tries to return more than has been received." If in examining our lives we can honestly tell ourselves that we work to give more, to serve more, to help more than we are given, served, or helped, then we are living in gratitude.

Think about Thomas Aquinas's gratitude "test" today. Do you try to return more than you receive?

—JAA

November 21

MY FATHER WAS A Baptist preacher in rural Mississippi. He had a favorite poem he quoted in his sermons from time to time. Here's an excerpt:

> Sunset and evening star,
>   And one clear call for me!
> And may there be no moaning of the bar,
>   When I put out to sea.
> Twilight and evening bell,
>   And after that the dark!
> And may there be no sadness of farewell,
>   When I embark . . .
> (From "Crossing the Bar" by Alfred, Lord Tennyson)

Dad recited this poem at his retirement service, and I recorded it. Years later, we played the recording at his funeral. I think everyone present was grateful to hear his voice again.

Have you had such life-affirming experiences for which you are grateful?

—JAA

November 22

"Humor is a prelude to faith and Laughter is the beginning of prayer."
(Reinhold Niebuhr)

HAVING GROWN UP IN a fundamentalist Christian environment, I was scared even to imply that anything having to do with God, faith, or prayer was funny. We just didn't laugh about those things. So I am particularly grateful by this liberating statement from Niebuhr. I find all kinds of things to laugh about in God's world.

Be grateful today for the gift of humor, laughter, and joy.

—JAA

November 23

"Friendship isn't a big thing—it's a million little things." (author unknown)

I AM GRATEFUL FOR many things my wife has taught me; high among those are all the little things a friend does, like remembering birthdays and sending cards, sending a note to a friend in the hospital, taking food when there's been a death in the family, phoning or sending an e-mail for no other reason than just staying in touch—in other words, making the extra effort to demonstrate gratitude for friendship by doing those "million little things."

How many of those little acts of friendship will you do today?

—JAA

November 24

WHAT'S YOUR FAVORITE TIME of day? I was asked that question but couldn't answer it because I couldn't make up my mind.

I love early mornings when I'm the only one up, have my coffee in hand, and can watch the sun rise and read the newspaper. I love winter sunsets when pink, blue, and purple stretch across the western sky and reflect on the snow. I love those nights when I lie in bed and let the rumble of distant thunder put me to sleep. I love rainy days, and I love sunny days. So I wonder how can there even be a favorite time of day. I can only conclude that I am grateful for any and every time of day.

Which time of this day are you most grateful for?

—JAA

November 25

I HAVE A KNIFE I've never used. I take it out of the box every once in a while and admire the workmanship. I don't mean the metal of the knife itself, but the beautifully crafted inlaid wood handle. It was a gift from my friend David Jordan, a man I worked with for many years. He is a master woodworker, though his arthritis no longer lets him do that work. Many times, I've been especially grateful for his friendship, and I'm sure he feels the same, though these days he often doesn't remember things. We had lunch recently, and he didn't remember giving me the knife. That's all the more reason I'm grateful for that knife, just as, over the years, I have been grateful for his friendship.

Surely you have old friends for whom you are grateful. Be in touch with at least one of them today.

—JAA

November 26

"Life without thankfulness is devoid of love and passion. Hope without thankfulness is lacking in fine perception. Faith without thankfulness lacks strength and fortitude. Every virtue divorced from thankfulness is maimed and limps along the spiritual road." (John Henry Jowett)

MR. JOWETT REMINDS US in the strongest terms that virtues practiced with gratitude are made stronger, while without gratitude they are "maimed."

Think today about how living with gratitude enhances every good thing you do and makes it even better.

—JAA

November 27

IT IS FUNNY HOW small things can symbolize such important milestones. For years, family gatherings around holidays were a mixed blessing with my stepson Jim. He invariably showed up late, ate with little or no conversation, and left the table to withdraw into another room where he would fall asleep for the rest of the afternoon.

That was before Jimmy found Alcoholics Anonymous. Now in recovery, Jim has been clean and sober for more than four years. What a difference it has made.

I think it hit me fully when, last Christmas, he asked me if he could bring a dish to the holiday dinner. "Sure," I said in disbelief, "that would be great." So he showed up, ahead of schedule, with a classic green bean casserole. The recipe was a favorite his mother used to prepare, and everyone loved it. And, of course, Jimmy was engaging and upbeat throughout dinner and the evening's activities.

I think the real Jimmy had been emerging from the effects of addiction for a long time, but somehow, the green bean casserole will always mark for me the point at which he returned to the family fold, sharing fully in the joys and obligations of family life.

Do some small events signify important growth in your life or the lives of those around you? Be grateful for these shared milestones.

—SJP

November 28

"Thanksgiving is good but thanks-living is better." (Matthew Henry)

WHAT I THINK MR. HENRY means is that it is one thing to feel thankful and another thing to live or act thankfully. After all, no one can know how we feel unless our feelings become behavior; no one can know we are thankful unless we show it. How? One simple way is by saying "thank you" to everyone who shows us generosity or kindness. Another is by being generous and kind ourselves.

Thanks-living? I can't think of a better way to describe living in gratitude. Can you?

—JAA

November 29

IN HIS BOOK, *Living Buddha, Living Christ*, Thich Nhat Hanh describes a Buddhist Thanksgiving: "On that day, we practice real gratitude—thanking our mothers, fathers, ancestors, friends, and all beings for everything." This reminds us that gratitude can't be limited; we must have enough gratitude to go around for everyone and everything that makes our lives better.

In this Thanksgiving season, make a list of all the people and things for which you are especially grateful.

—JAA

November 30

I BELIEVE IN CHRISTMAS miracles. I experience one every year about this time.

On the weekend following Thanksgiving, we customarily put up our holiday decorations. We have a twenty-year old artificial tree that is slowly but surely dropping its artificial needles. Still, each year we pull it out of the box, thinking this will be its last.

Our son Ronald joins us for the ritual tree trimming and has become especially proficient at assembling the tree. Jim is the master of stringing the lights, occasionally swearing at burned-out bulbs as he goes.

Once the lights are on, we all join in adorning the tree with our odd assortment of ornaments. We have accumulated scores of them over the years. Some are simple handmade ornaments from Ronald's early school years. There's an angel made from cotton bolls from a Mississippi farm, a small painted gourd Jim's mother made, some starched, tatted snowflakes my mother crocheted, a dozen ceramic and wooden painted birds we collected over the years, and some old-fashioned shiny red and gold ornaments that have seen better days.

Each year, we open the boxes of stored ornaments, stare at this jumble of ragtag items, and wonder how we can possibly make our tree presentable with this pitiful menagerie.

But we forge ahead, trimming the tree together while we listen to Christmas tunes and sip eggnog.

And then it happens—the Christmas miracle. The finished tree is magnificent, and the motley collection of ornaments is now mysteriously beautiful to behold.

What simple holiday traditions in your life are transformed into miracles through eyes of gratitude?

—SJP

December 1

BEGIN THIS MONTH WITH gratitude for love—love of family, love of friends, love of our faith, love of ourselves, and love of all with whom we share this world.

There have been millions of words written about love. Here are a few:

"There was never any yet that wholly could escape love, and never shall there be any, never so long as beauty shall be, never so long as eyes can see." (Longus)

"Love never faileth." (1 Corinthians 13:8)

"Neither a lofty degree of intelligence nor imagination nor both together go to the making of genius. Love, love, love, that is the soul of genius." (Mozart)

"He that loveth not, knoweth not God; for God is love." (John, Holy Bible)

"We love the things we love for what they are." (Robert Frost)

"What is life without the radiance of love?" (Schiller)

Now take a few minutes and write a note of gratitude for the love in your life.

—JAA

December 2

WHEN MY SONS WERE little, my routine for tucking them into bed was to cover them comfortably, then lie on top of them (not with my full weight) and pretend to "smush" them into the bed. I'd say "smuu-uhhhsh, smuuuuhhhsh," dragging out the words for full effect. Pretending to struggle, they'd cry, "Stop, stop," then giggle. Thus, being thoroughly "smushed" into the bed, they'd settle down for the night. One son, Rick, became a good weaver in his adolescent days and made some beautiful things, one of which he gave me as a surprise birthday present. It hangs now in my bedroom, is about the width of a belt, and is red with these words in blue: "The Master Smusher." How could I not be grateful?

Do you have such personal mementos for which you are grateful?

—JAA

December 3

FORMER COLLEAGUE MIKE HOOD wrote to me with a moving gratitude story: "Nan," he said, "had to write many gratitude lists to stay sober and sane."

Nan was a friend of his and of many other people in the recovery community in our city. She urged everyone she knew to make a gratitude list. And she set the example. She'd say, "I've got to get out Old Yellar," referring to an 8 1/2-by-14-inch legal pad, "and go to work." She has been dead for fifteen years, but her friends still preach the benefits of "Old Yellar."

Mike says she taught them a trick for how to start a gratitude list: "Write the alphabet down the left side of 'Old Yellar,'" she instructed. Mike concludes, "Worked for me. I've been sober twenty-nine years."

I suspect that trick would work for all of us, and I'm grateful to Mike for sharing it.

—JAA

December 4

EVERY YEAR IN EARLY December, my mother makes a huge batch of special holiday cookies and distributes tins of them to all her children and grandchildren. The recipe is one that circulated in my small hometown almost fifty years ago, and it has become a real Christmas tradition in our family.

These special spice cookies require pounds of dried fruits, like raisins and dates, that must be put through a meat grinder before mixing them with flour, sugar, and spices. The cookie dough has to be rolled out and cut into rounds, then baked, cooled, and frosted with a thin glaze. My father gets into the act as the official grinder—and helps with the cleanup, too. They bake dozens and dozens of cookies, so this is no small undertaking.

My sister and I remember baking these cookies when were young and expect to do so for our own families again someday. But right now, we enjoy with great anticipation this annual gift of love from our parents' kitchen.

Christmas time is about anticipation, love, and joy. Are you grateful for the gifts of love that arrive daily?

—SJP

December 5

"Reflect upon your present blessings, of which every [person] has plenty; not on your past misfortunes, of which all [people] have some." (Charles Dickens)

IT'S IMPORTANT TO ADMIT mistakes, to express regret, and to ask forgiveness. It is just as important to then put the mistakes in your past, forget about them, let them go, and not let them haunt you. I learned a while ago that it's easy to build up a whole life of "if onlys"—and that it is the most destructive thing I could do. Better by far to face my mistakes and failures, put them behind me, and turn my mind to my blessings and to living in gratitude.

Are there regrets or mistakes you need to put behind you and forget about while you work to live a life of gratitude?

—JAA

December 6

I HAVE A CLOSE friend who managed to survive a painful and life-threatening medical problem. After his recovery, he vowed to spend more time with the people he loved. He told me, "I don't want to look back ten years from now and say, 'I wanted so much to spend time with so-and-so who is now dead. One thing you learn on your deathbed, which is where I thought I was, is that this life is about loving and serving others and taking time to do it." Clearly, this is the way he has chosen to express his gratitude for just being alive.

You certainly don't have to be near death to show your appreciation every day for those you love. You can do that today.

—JAA

CHOOSING GRATITUDE

December 7

AFTER A RECENT SNOWSTORM, I phoned Pete, my ninety-two-year-old father-in-law, to see how many inches of snow his town had received. He is a World War II veteran, a retired businessman, and a man of great humor and sunny outlook. It always gives me a gratitude fix to talk with him. On this call, he would not let me hang up until he shared a snowstorm joke:

> Lena: "Sven, the snow ordinance is in effect, the snow plows are coming, and you have to park on the side of the street with even house numbers."
>
> The next day, Lena said, "Sven, you have to park on the side of the street with odd house numbers."
>
> Then the next day, she said, "Sven, they've lifted the parking restrictions so tomorrow you can park in our garage."

Pete and I shared a laugh together and said our good-byes. Not a new joke, to be sure, but it gave me a lift on a day of snow-shoveling and slick streets.

If your sense of gratitude is lagging, why not try a dose of humor? It doesn't even have to be all that funny.

—JAA

December 8

I'M A MEMBER OF a city church with a large, impressive sanctuary. We're in the midst of doing some maintenance, repair, and remodeling. One of the most important changes, in my opinion, is a substantial modification to the chancel area that will incorporate an elegantly designed ramp.

I am always grateful for people who create ways to accommodate those with disabilities.

—JAA

December 9

I REMEMBER THE DAYS when people with disabilities were kept on the margins of society. Now they are brought into the mainstream in many ways. I'm grateful for the laws that support and make that possible. I'm grateful for the educators who prepare those children and young people to be the most they can be. I'm grateful for the inventors and manufacturers of prosthesis devices of all kinds. I'm grateful for the researchers who spend their lives trying to find better medications and devices. I could go on and on and not exhaust the list of people doing this noble work. And of course I'm grateful for the courage and determination of the people themselves with disabilities.

Surely you know someone, perhaps a loved one, who lives a better life because of all this work. Be grateful for that today.

—JAA

December 10

"He enjoys much who is thankful for little; a grateful mind is both a great and a happy mind." (Thomas Secker, 1693–1768, Archbishop of Canterbury)

ONE OF THE JOYS of writing this book has been researching what others have said about gratitude over the centuries. I am constantly reminded by these wise souls that what I have is enough, and I should be grateful for that sufficiency.

Think about what you have. Is it enough? Do you have a great and happy mind today?

—JAA

December 11

AS WITH ALL COUPLES, our marriage has had its bumps along the way. Following a serious crisis in our relationship last summer, we planted a special tree in our front yard. It's a daily reminder of our faith in the future and our commitment to continue to nurture and grow in our love for one another.

On a recent winter evening, my husband called me to look out our front door. The sun was low in the western sky, its long rays striking the red bark Japanese maple and visually setting it afire. The bare red branches feathered skyward like a flame. We silently hugged one another.

Gratitude is not always about the goods things that happen to us. Life, after all, is a bumpy road.

—SJP

December 12

THE AUTHOR OF *Zorba the Greek* wrote often about seeking or seeing God appearing in different forms. He wrote, "I said to the almond tree, 'Speak to me of God,' and the almond tree blossomed." If I let go of my preconceptions and preoccupations and open myself to gratitude, I am able to see the Divine not only in people but also in all the forms of nature, from clouds to birds to blossoms.

Really look and be open today, and you will be able to see the Divine in a loved one, in your garden, or even in yourself.

—JAA

December 13

"God gave you a gift of 86,400 seconds today. Have you used one to say, 'Thank you'?" (William A. Ward)

WELL, HAVE YOU? Here's a suggestion for right now: Go to Facebook, Twitter, LinkedIn, or e-mail and send a message of thanks to your various and sundry friends and contacts. But that's not nearly personal enough. Next, pick up the phone (or take it out of your pocket) and make personal contact with someone to whom you can or should or want to say *thank you.*

Then, you can answer Mr. Ward's question with a resounding "Yes!"

—JAA

December 14

On this anniversary of the tragedy in Newtown, I choose to remember a story about one teacher and one classroom at Sandy Hook Elementary School.

Kaitlin Roig had taught first grade for six years at Sandy Hook. When the gunfire started, she ushered her fifteen frightened students into a three-foot-square bathroom, slid a storage cabinet in front of the door, slipped inside, locked the door, and turned out the light.

Huddled there, they heard the gunfire from the hallway and the other side of the bathroom wall.

"I thought we were all going to die," Kaitlin said, "so I told the children how special they were to me and that I loved them. I wanted the last words each one heard to be 'I love you.'"

Kaitlin kept the children there safely until the police arrived.

Even in the midst of tragedy and violence, we can be grateful for the courage and wisdom of those who remember the power of love.

—SJP

December 15

I BELIEVE THAT OUR role in life is not to judge and approve or disapprove of others, but to accept them as they are. Obviously, I don't include people who do destructive or criminal things; I'm talking about people of different beliefs, people who have habits we find irritating, or people with whom we simply disagree. Our church has a motto or slogan or statement of principle that I think could apply to every organization on earth, from churches to social clubs to businesses and even to families: "We agree to differ, we resolve to love, we unite to serve."

If it were up to me, I'd put that in the Constitution; barring that, I'm still very grateful that it is part of our church.

What statements or principles or simple sayings are you grateful for?

—JAA

December 16

IT SNOWED SEVEN INCHES last night. I arose at 6 A.M. and cranked up the snow blower and thought, "I am grateful for this snow blower." But it wasn't because I didn't have to shovel snow in the old-fashioned way; it was because I think of the snow blower almost the way a sculptor thinks of his or her tools. I have a certain way I move the snow, and I have an image of how I want the driveway and sidewalks to look when I'm done. I know it sounds a little compulsive, but it gives me a rewarding sense of accomplishment.

And, oh yes, I'm also grateful for the snow.

Can you find gratitude for what other people call inconveniences?

—JAA

December 17

MY FATHER BELIEVED THERE was good in everyone, and as a minister he was often challenged to maintain that optimism. Once he was asked to conduct a funeral for a woman with a bad reputation in the community. There were people in his church who thought he shouldn't do it because, after all, "What could he ever say good about her?" But Dad's commitment to his calling as a minister compelled him to assure a dignified and appropriate service and burial for the woman, regardless of community attitudes. In the South of that day, there were preachers who were known to "preach a person into Hell" by turning the funeral message into a litany of the person's "sins," and some people wondered if Dad would do that. But those people didn't know my father. His sermon was generous; he found good things to say, and he honored her family.

"I know I disappointed some folks," Dad told me, "because they couldn't see anything good about _____, but if you look closely enough, you can find the good in most everyone."

I sincerely believe that to be true, and the more experience I have, I realize that when we're looking for the good in others, we're really looking for the Divine spark within them. I know that woman's family was grateful for Dad's message of love.

Be grateful for the Divine spark within us, and resolve to look for it in others.

—JAA

December 18

AT OUR CHURCH'S SATURDAY night informal worship service, we have a practice of sharing joys and concerns to be lifted in prayer. Last year as the Catholic Cardinals were meeting in the Vatican to elect a new Pope, one of our members asked that we pray for the Cardinals' wisdom and discernment.

The request took this liberal Protestant by surprise. I had to admit to myself my own cynical view that the election of a new Pope was more politics than religion. At that moment, I realized that I should have more faith in God's power to be at work in every situation and, perhaps first, in my own heart.

What prejudice or cynicism do you need to examine? Are you grateful when others expose your shortcomings?

—SJP

December 19

"For every minute you are angry, you lose sixty seconds of happiness."
(Ralph Waldo Emerson)

I CAN'T IMAGINE HOW many seconds of happiness I have lost because I let my temper get the best of me. I'm happy to say that I'm not nearly as bad as I used to be and have learned—most of the time—to step back, take a deep breath, and be grateful for all my emotions, even anger. That way, gratitude becomes like a meditation.

Be grateful for all your emotions today, and if you're angry, breathe deeply and try to let your gratitude overcome the anger.

—JAA

December 20

"Never say there is nothing beautiful in the world anymore. There is always something to make you wonder in the shape of a tree, the trembling of a leaf." (Albert Schweitzer)

WE HAVE SOME DREARY days in the city where I live in Iowa, and sometimes in the middle of winter it's difficult to find beauty. At the beginning of winter the first snow is always beautiful, but after several snows and hours of clearing the driveway and sidewalks, the mixture of grit and exhaust soot settles on everything, and it seems that nothing looks beautiful. It even becomes difficult to make a gratitude list. And yet beauty is there if we forget the inconveniences and look closer. Our winter sunsets are the most beautiful, and their pink and blue and golden light even colors the dirty snow. The birds in their various colors still gather at the feeder. And there's joy in watching children sledding on the golf course. We are still surrounded by sources of gratitude.

Can you live in gratitude and still find beauty in the world today?

—JAA

December 21

IN RESPONDING TO MY previous book, *Choosing Gratitude*, a friend wrote with his list of goals. He said, "The virtues I must pay more attention to are fidelity, prudence, temperance, humility, simplicity, purity, gentleness, and good faith." He added, "Now there's a challenge."

Yes, that's a challenge, but I'm grateful on his behalf that he has taken the first difficult step simply by identifying how he wants to be.

Have you set for yourself certain goals of virtue? If so, understand that the most important step toward accomplishing them is to live in gratitude every day.

—JAA

CHOOSING GRATITUDE

December 22

I HAVE A CARTOON on my bulletin board, taken from an old magazine some years ago. In it, a rather hapless looking man is facing St. Peter, who is saying, "No, no, that's not a sin either. My goodness, you must have worried yourself to death." This little bit of humor is a daily reminder to worry less about the ways I've failed to do what I should have done, and to be more grateful for the things I've done right and the opportunities I continue to have.

Take time today to do a little inventory of the things you have done, and continue to do, right. Then be grateful for the time you still have to do things right.

—JAA

December 23

MY BROTHER, DENNY, IS a very successful businessman and a man of great personal generosity, but he prides himself on negotiating a bargain or saving a dollar.

Several years ago, he got one of his famous bargains by purchasing a large inventory of birdhouses made of birdseed that for some unexplained reason seemed never to attract birds. He didn't have any outlet for selling the birdhouses, so for several years he gleefully boxed and wrapped them as gag gifts for family members at Christmas. The prank became a running joke, and he seemed to relish the abuse the rest of us heaped on him for his rather odd annual Scrooge-like gifts.

Those birdhouses provided lots of good-natured teasing and memorable laughter during the holidays. Perhaps they were a good investment, after all.

Do your fondest memories often attach to the unusual or colorful antics or personalities of friends or family members? Be grateful for people who make life's experiences worthy of recounting again and again.

—SJP

December 24

CHRISTMAS MEMORY

We went to church and sang carols
and sometimes acted out the baby Jesus story
using old sheets and robes to be wise men and shepherds.
And the preacher said
wouldn't it be nice if we could keep
the spirit of Christmas all year long.
And we thought it would be nice
and told ourselves we'd try.
(from *Nights Under a Tin Roof*)

This is a good day to be grateful for your own Christmas memories.

—JAA

December 25

"In every child who is born, the potentiality of the human race is born again . . . the utmost idea of goodness . . . and of God." (James Agee)

PERHAPS THIS DAY MORE than any other day we should stop to think about the potential of every single child. And, we should honor that possibility by being sure the opportunity exists for every child to blossom.

May we see the potential for the human race in the face of every child and be grateful.

—SJP

December 26

A MINISTER FRIEND, PAUL Johnson, says that he often offers this observation to people who say they want life to be happier and more joyful: "It is impossible to invent 'joy' out of nothing, but if you want to be happier and more joyful, focus on the things you are grateful for."

Take Paul's advice and focus today on the things for which you are grateful. Then enjoy the happiness that results.

—JAA

December 27

MY EARLY CHURCH EXPERIENCES, it seems to me, were more about fear than they were about faith. It was as if the preachers were trying to scare everyone into believing. I suspect it worked on a lot of people; it worked on me for a while. I'm grateful that I was able to grow into a better view of the connection with God. I submit that fear is never going to be a great motivator for religious faith, devotion, and worship, just as it is not a great motivator in human relationships. After all, the Scripture doesn't say, "God is fear." It says, "God is love."

Are you grateful today for the power of love in your life?

—JAA

December 28

"Gratitude is not only the greatest of virtues, but the parent of all the others." (Marcus Tullius Cicero)

THINK ABOUT IT. Any virtue you can name flows from a spirit of gratitude. Generosity? The grateful person accepts that what he or she has is enough, thus is generous with others. Compassion? The grateful person, feeling his or her own blessings, is compassionate with those who are not so blessed. That's what Cicero means by "the parent of all the others."

Make a note of the virtues at the beginning of each chapter (month) in this book, and examine how gratitude makes each of them more meaningful.

—JAA

December 29

I WAS FORTUNATE ENOUGH to work with several people who had a way of lifting everyone's spirits. One of them, for whom I was particularly grateful, was a copy editor who, most of the time, worked quietly and unobtrusively. Our editorial group regularly had parties or end-of-the day get-togethers of one sort or another. When at those gatherings, our copy editor friend was asked how he was, he would reply with great exuberance, "I'm ready to lay aside the cares of the day and let mirth reign unrestrained." What a great way to end the day.

Do you have a friend or acquaintance who lifts your spirits? Be grateful for that person.

—JAA

December 30

THE CHRISTIAN MYSTIC MEISTER ECKHART wrote, "In praying it is enough to say 'thank you.'" Too many times I find myself asking for something rather than just saying, "Thank you." And of course, feeling and expressing gratitude is the central message of this whole book.

Say "thank you" today, to God, to a loved one, to a friend, to the bus driver, to a policeman, to a teacher, to a minister, to a community volunteer, to a store clerk, to a health care worker, to a person who lets you help him or her—and to yourself.

—JAA

December 31

"When life gives you a hundred reasons to cry, show life that you have a thousand reasons to smile." (Shing Xiong)

WE CAN'T THINK OF A better sentiment with which to end this book of days. There's always a little sadness on New Year's Eve; that's probably why people have parties and create an atmosphere of laughter and good times. If we're not careful, we'll find ourselves looking back on all the things that went wrong in the world and on all the things we didn't get done this year rather than celebrating the things that went well and that we did get done. So, like a lot of people, we are grateful for the parties and good times that help us lay aside the cares of the year and let "mirth reign unrestrained."

Will you join us in greeting the new year with joy and gratitude?

—JAA & SJP

About the Authors

James A. Autry is the author of eleven books, the most recent of which was 2012's *Choosing Gratitude: Learning to Love the Life You Have*. A former Fortune 500 executive and magazine editor, he now writes, lectures, and conducts workshops on Servant Leadership in this country and internationally. For one academic year, he held an endowed chair in leadership at Iowa State University and holds four honorary degrees. He describes this collaboration with his wife, Sally Pederson, as a great joy and hopes that spirit shines through the book itself.

Sally J. Pederson is an advocate for children and adults with disabilities and a voice for progressive causes. She served as Lieutenant Governor of Iowa from 1999 to 2007 and is a former editor with *Better Homes & Gardens* magazine, where she met and married the love of her life, Jim Autry.

She is founding president of The Homestead, a non-profit agency serving people with autism, and founding chair of REACH, a college program for students with multiple learning disabilities at the University of Iowa. She has served on numerous boards, including the National Alliance for Autism Research (now Autism Speaks) and the Union Theological Seminary in New York. Currently, she serves as a director of the Northwest Area Foundation in St. Paul, Minnesota, and on the Advisory Board of the Harkin Institute for Public Policy & Civic Engagement at Drake University in Des Moines. This is her first book.